MW00907667

Published by TechEd Maven Consulting, LLC
www.TechEdMaven.com
Cover design by TechEd, Maven Consulting LLC
ISBN: E-Book TBD
ISBN: **9798397292900**

This eBook is for educational purposes only. The information contained within is intended to assist and inspire readers, but the author makes no representations or warranties with respect to the accuracy or completeness of the contents. The author shall not be liable for any loss or damages arising from the use of this eBook.

Liability Release:
By reading this eBook, you acknowledge that the author is not responsible for any outcomes or consequences resulting from the implementation of the strategies, suggestions, or techniques discussed. The reader assumes full responsibility for their actions and releases the author from any liability.

Trademark Notice:
All trademarks mentioned in this eBook belong to their respective owners and are used for identification purposes only. The use of such trademarks does not imply any affiliation with or endorsement by the trademark owners.

Series Introduction

Welcome to the **A.C.E. E-Book Series™** - a set of comprehensive guides to leverage the power of Artificial Intelligence & Chat GPT to empower you to A.C.E. your game as an educator. Whether you're in your first five years of teaching or a seasoned educator aiming to enhance your teaching and leadership practices, this series is designed to provide you with tools and strategies to help you excel in your practice - using Artificial Intelligence as your ultimate cheat code.

Accelerate: With over 250 prompts and dialogues, unleash the power of Chat GPT to accelerate your success. Discover AI prompts that provide instant insights, time-saving strategies, and innovative approaches to fast-track your professional growth and student outcomes. With Chat GPT as your trusted companion, you can access a wealth of knowledge and resources to propel your teaching effectiveness to new heights - while you learn how to A.C.E. your evaluations.

Crush: Crush your teaching goals with Chat GPT as your ultimate cheat code. Decode effective teaching practices, overcome evaluation challenges, and unlock hidden strategies that will help you conquer your evaluations and excel in the classroom. First we will learn to utilize Chat GPT to A.C.E. your evaluations by aligning your teaching practices to demystify and crush common evaluation frameworks and maximize your impact on student learning.

Elevate: Elevate your teaching practices to new heights with Chat GPT as your guiding force. Access cutting-edge resources, personalized recommendations, and AI-driven insights that align with common best practices in teaching. Discover how Chat GPT can empower you to elevate your instructional strategies, engage your students effectively, and create an exceptional learning environment that reflects the expectations of your evaluations. By incorporating AI prompts into your teaching approach, you can A.C.E. your evaluations and take your teaching to the next level.

Join us in this transformative journey as we dive into the A.C.E. E-Book Series. Accelerate your growth, crush your challenges, and elevate your teaching practices to A.C.E. your craft as an educator. With Chat GPT as your invaluable resource, you'll have the guidance and support you need to unlock your full potential and become an even more exceptional educator. It's time to A.C.E. your way to success with Chat GPT!

Table of Contents

Prequel

Ethical Foundations for Harnessing the Power of AI in Education

Introduction: Ethical Leadership in Harnessing the Power of AI

While this may be one of the shortest Episodes in this book, it is undeniably the most important, and I urge you to refer back to it regularly. As educators, you are at the forefront of a transformative era where Artificial Intelligence (AI) is reshaping the educational landscape. However, this transformation must be guided by ethical considerations, a commitment to equity, and a steadfast focus on keeping "Humans in the Loop."

The U.S. Department of Education, Office of Educational Technology, in its 2023 report The Future of Artificial Intelligence in Teaching and Learning - emphasizes the importance of a Human-in-the-Loop (HITL) approach, stating that "people are part of the process of noticing patterns in an educational system and assigning meaning to those patterns. It also means that teachers remain at the helm of major instructional decisions" (p. 17). This vision of AI ensures that educators are not replaced but rather solidified as central figures in instructional decision-making, reinforcing "the responsibility of teachers to exercise judgment and control over the use of AI in education" p. 54).

The HITL concept extends beyond the classroom, encompassing three critical loops: moment-to-moment teaching decisions, planning and reflection, and participation in the design, selection, and evaluation of AI-enabled technologies (U.S. Department of Education, Office of Educational Technology, 2023, p. 29). These loops underscore the multifaceted role of educators in shaping the future of AI in education.

Equity and the avoidance of bias are paramount. As the report warns, "Equity, of course, is one of those priorities that requires constant attention, especially given the worrisome consequences of potentially biased AI models" (p. 54). As educators, you must be vigilant in ensuring that AI technologies are implemented with fairness and inclusivity at their core.

This prequel will guide you through best practices and strategies for harnessing the power of AI responsibly and ethically. It will provide insights into establishing productive relationships with AI tools, structuring conversations for optimal outcomes, incorporating AI feedback into teaching practice, and overcoming challenges and limitations. Above all, it will emphasize the importance of personal identifying information and student privacy, aligning with the ethical guidelines and your school's policies.

Together, we will explore how to leverage AI to enhance teaching and learning while maintaining a human-centered approach that prioritizes ethics, equity, and the essential role of educators.

Child Safety and Ethical Considerations in AI Integration

In the era of AI-driven education, the safety and privacy of our students remain paramount. As educators, we must be vigilant in adhering to ethical guidelines and legal regulations that govern the use of technology in the classroom. The Children's Online Privacy Protection Rule (COPPA) provides essential insights that align with our commitment to responsible AI integration - Please review and file away for your reference.

Protection of Personal Information: COPPA emphasizes the importance of protecting the "confidentiality, security, and integrity of personal information collected from children" (16 CFR Part 312, p. 10). As educators, we must ensure that AI tools are implemented with robust security measures, safeguarding our students' personal information.

Parental Rights and Consent: Transparency and collaboration with parents are vital. COPPA outlines the rights of parents to review and control the personal information provided by their children, requiring operators to obtain verifiable parental consent (16 CFR Part 312, p. 9). School leaders must foster open communication with parents, ensuring they are informed and actively involved in decisions related to AI integration.

Prohibition against Unnecessary Collection: We must adhere to the principle of minimal data collection, as COPPA prohibits operators from conditioning a child's participation on the disclosure of more personal information than is reasonably necessary (16 CFR Part 312, p. 10). This guideline reinforces our responsibility to limit the collection of student data to what is essential for educational purposes.

Data Retention and Deletion Requirements: COPPA emphasizes the importance of retaining personal information only for as long as necessary and ensuring secure deletion (16 CFR Part 312, p. 10). Schools must establish clear protocols for data retention and deletion, reflecting our commitment to privacy and security. No identifying or confidential information should ever be entered into Chat-GPT or any AI program that is not specifically governed by the policies and permissions of your specific district.

Our role as educator extends beyond compliance; we are key stakeholders in shaping a responsible and innovative educational environment. By adhering to these principles, we ensure that AI integration aligns with our core values, fostering a culture of trust, responsibility, and human-centered innovation.

Recognizing and Addressing Potential Biases in AI Outputs: A Leadership Perspective

AI tools like ChatGPT offer powerful insights and support, but it's crucial to recognize and address the potential biases that may arise from their outputs. These biases can stem from the inherent biased characteristics of the internet, which often represents a Western point of view and is largely in English. Additionally, biases may be present in AI detectors, particularly in non-native speaking individuals, and should be avoided.

Understanding the source of bias: Generative AI platforms draw inputs from the internet, which can inherently carry biases. As educators it's essential to understand that these biases may reflect in AI-generated content. The Future of Artificial Intelligence in Teaching and Learning - highlights the importance of recognizing these biases and taking appropriate measures to address them.

Human in the Loop: Emphasizing the importance of human judgment and critical evaluation is vital. Encourage teachers and students to critically evaluate AI-generated content, identifying potential biases, and making informed decisions. Human expertise should always complement AI tools, ensuring that the content aligns with diverse perspectives and ethical considerations.

Educating Staff and Students: Attend and lead professional development and educational programs that teach staff and students to recognize and address biases in AI outputs. Refer back to The Future of Artificial Intelligence in Teaching and Learning for insights that can be integrated into these programs.

Promoting Critical Thinking and Ethical Considerations: Aligning with the revised Bloom's Taxonomy and Depth of Knowledge (DOK), foster a culture that promotes critical thinking, evaluation, and ethical considerations. Encourage teachers and students to engage in higher-level thinking skills such as evaluating, critiquing, and differentiating, as outlined in the "Evaluate" and "Analyze" stages of the revised Bloom's Taxonomy and DOK-3 (Knowledge Analysis).

By recognizing and addressing potential biases in AI outputs, educational leaders can guide teachers and students in leveraging AI tools responsibly and ethically. Emphasizing human judgment, promoting critical thinking, and implementing educational programs that focus on recognizing biases are essential strategies to ensure that AI tools like ChatGPT are used effectively and responsibly in the educational environment.

Now.... Let's get to the prompts....

Episode One
<u>Preparatory Protocols</u>

Understanding the Components of Preparatory Protocols

Preparing and Planning is crucial to your success as a teacher and that encompasses many elements that we will share how to A.C.E.! As educators across different grade levels and subjects, teachers A.C.E. unique challenges in understanding and effectively delivering the content they are charged with teaching and pedagogy (practice of teaching). ChatGPT can serve as a valuable resource for teachers at all grade levels, from Pre-Kindergarten through doctoral level instructors..

Content Understanding and Clarity:
ChatGPT can help teachers gain a deeper understanding of content across different subjects and grade levels. For example, if a high school math teacher needs clarification on a complex algebraic concept, they can engage with ChatGPT to receive explanations, examples, and step-by-step problem-solving strategies specific to that topic. Similarly, an elementary school science teacher can seek guidance from ChatGPT to explain scientific phenomena in simple terms and explore age-appropriate activities to engage young learners.

Subject-Specific Pedagogy:
ChatGPT can assist teachers in understanding subject-specific pedagogy by offering instructional strategies, teaching methods, and resources tailored to different grade levels and content areas. Whether it's providing guidance on differentiated instruction for a diverse classroom or suggesting interactive learning tools for a language arts lesson, ChatGPT can offer valuable insights to support effective teaching practices.

Adaptability and Personalization:
Teachers can engage in interactive conversations with ChatGPT to address the specific needs of their students. By providing information about the learners' grade level, abilities, and background, teachers can receive tailored recommendations and exemplars from ChatGPT that align with their students' unique requirements. For instance, an elementary school teacher seeking strategies to support English language learners can receive guidance on language acquisition techniques and access resources designed specifically for their students' language development.

By utilizing ChatGPT as a tool for content and pedagogical understanding, teachers can access a wide range of resources, including exemplars, instructional materials, and real-life examples. These resources can help teachers clarify complex concepts, explore alternative approaches to instruction, and discover new ideas to engage students in their learning.

Example Prompts/Dialogue:

Teacher: "ChatGPT, I'm teaching fractions to my fourth-grade students. Can you provide me with some exemplars or visual representations to help them understand this concept better?"

ChatGPT: "Certainly! Here are some exemplars you can use: *[GPT provides examples of visual representations, word problems, and manipulatives].* These exemplars are designed specifically for fourth-grade students and can help them grasp the concept of fractions effectively."

Through the collaborative interaction with ChatGPT, teachers can enhance their content knowledge, explore pedagogical strategies, and access a wealth of resources suitable for diverse grade levels and subjects. This empowers teachers to deliver instruction that is aligned with their school and district's expectations and promotes meaningful learning experiences for their students.

Remember, ChatGPT is a valuable tool that can support teachers in their professional growth by providing subject-specific guidance, personalized resources, and adaptable strategies. By leveraging ChatGPT's capabilities, educators can deepen their understanding of content and pedagogy, resulting in improved instruction and enhanced student outcomes across various grade levels in PK-20 education.

Interpreting The Indicators And Expectations

When engaging in planning and preparation, teachers are expected to interpret the indicators and expectations outlined within various evaluative frameworks. This involves understanding the specific criteria and performance levels against which their teaching will be evaluated. ChatGPT can be a valuable tool for teachers to gain a deeper understanding of these indicators and expectations, enabling them to better prepare for their evaluations, no matter what framework is being used in their evaluation..

Clarifying Indicator Language:

The language used in the indicators and expectations of evaluation frameworks may sometimes be complex or open to interpretation. ChatGPT can assist teachers in deciphering this language and providing explanations in more accessible terms. By engaging in interactive dialogues, teachers can ask ChatGPT for clarification on specific indicators and receive simplified explanations that enhance their understanding. For instance:

Example Prompts/Dialogue:

Teacher: "ChatGPT, I'm a third-grade science teacher, and I'm having trouble understanding what 'evidence-based reasoning' means in the context of scientific investigations. Can you help me clarify this?"

ChatGPT: "Certainly! 'Evidence-based reasoning' refers to the process of using scientific evidence to support claims or explanations. In third grade, this can involve students gathering data, making observations, and using that evidence to draw conclusions or make predictions. Here are some age-appropriate activities you can incorporate to develop students' evidence-based reasoning skills."

Example Prompts/Dialogue:

Teacher: "ChatGPT, I teach high school social studies, and I'm unsure about the expectations for 'evaluating multiple perspectives' when analyzing historical events. Can you explain this indicator in more accessible terms?"

ChatGPT: "Certainly! 'Evaluating multiple perspectives' means considering various viewpoints and interpretations when examining historical events. In your high school class, this can involve analyzing primary and secondary sources, considering different cultural or ideological perspectives, and discussing how these perspectives shape our understanding of history. Here are some strategies and resources to help your students engage in evaluating multiple perspectives."

Providing Examples and Exemplars:

To further support teachers in comprehending the indicators and expectations, ChatGPT can offer examples and exemplars that demonstrate each performance level. By engaging in conversations with ChatGPT, teachers can explore scenarios and receive guidance on how to meet the different performance levels outlined in the framework. ChatGPT can provide practical examples of instructional strategies, lesson plans, and classroom activities that align with each level of performance. This helps teachers develop a clearer understanding of the expectations and enables them to identify areas for growth and improvement.

Example Prompts/Dialogue:

Teacher: "ChatGPT, I'm an elementary math teacher, and I'm looking for examples of how to incorporate hands-on manipulatives to teach fractions effectively to my second-grade students."

ChatGPT: "Certainly! Second-grade students can benefit from hands-on activities such as using fraction bars, fraction circles, or even everyday objects like pizza slices to explore fractions. Here are some specific activities and lesson ideas you can try in your classroom to help your students develop a solid understanding of fractions."

Example Prompts/Dialogue:

Teacher: "ChatGPT, I'm a high school English teacher, and I'm searching for exemplars that demonstrate effective use of textual evidence in literary analysis essays. Can you provide some examples to guide my instruction?"

ChatGPT: "Certainly! When analyzing literature, high school students can strengthen their arguments by citing specific textual evidence and providing insightful interpretations. Here are some exemplars of strong textual analysis essays, including the use of direct quotations, analysis of literary devices, and clear connections between evidence and the student's argument. These exemplars can serve as models for your students and help them understand the expectations for incorporating textual evidence in their own literary analyses."

Interactive Reflection:

ChatGPT can facilitate reflective dialogue with teachers, allowing them to interact with specific indicators and expectations based on their own instructional practices. By engaging in conversations about their teaching experiences, teachers can seek feedback and guidance from ChatGPT on how to improve their instructional strategies and align them with the framework. For example:

Example Prompts/Dialogue:

Teacher: "ChatGPT, I teach elementary physical education, and I'm working on incorporating more inclusive practices during my lessons. Can you provide suggestions on how I can better accommodate students with diverse abilities?"

ChatGPT: "Certainly! Inclusive practices in physical education involve providing modifications, adaptations, and alternative activities to ensure all students can participate and succeed. Here are some strategies and resources that can help you create an inclusive and supportive environment for students with diverse abilities."

Example Prompts/Dialogue:

Teacher: "ChatGPT, as a high school Spanish teacher, I want to enhance my students' cultural understanding. How can I engage them in authentic conversations and interactions?"

ChatGPT: "That's great! Authentic conversations and interactions can be fostered by incorporating real-world scenarios, cultural artifacts, and role-playing activities. I can provide you with specific examples and ideas to create meaningful cultural exchanges in your Spanish classroom, enabling your students to develop a deeper understanding of the language and its cultural context."

By utilizing ChatGPT as a resource for interpreting the indicators and expectations, teachers can gain clarity and insights into what is being asked of them in their evaluations. The interactive nature of ChatGPT allows teachers to engage in dialogue, seek clarification, and receive specific guidance tailored to their instructional context. This empowers teachers to align their instructional practices with the expectations of the framework their administrators are utilizing and to improve their overall teaching effectiveness.

Remember, ChatGPT can assist teachers in interpreting the language, providing examples, and engaging in interactive reflection related to the indicators and expectations of various evaluation frameworks. By utilizing ChatGPT as a tool for understanding, teachers can enhance their preparation for evaluations and make informed decisions to further their professional growth and instructional practice.

Using Chat Gpt To Clarify Preparation And Planning Requirements

When engaging in preparation and planning activities, teachers are expected to demonstrate an understanding of the requirements for effective lesson planning and instructional preparation. ChatGPT can be a valuable resource for teachers to clarify these requirements and gain a deeper understanding of what the framework is asking of them.

Accessing Standards:
ChatGPT can assist teachers in accessing the standards and guidelines specific to their grade level and subject area. By providing information about the desired standards, teachers can engage with ChatGPT to obtain the necessary documentation, official frameworks, or curriculum guides that outline the learning goals and expectations for their students. For instance, a middle school English teacher can inquire about the Common Core State Standards for reading literature, and ChatGPT can provide a comprehensive breakdown of the standards, including specific skills and concepts to address.

Sequencing Standards:
Once teachers have accessed the standards, ChatGPT can help them sequence the standards effectively to create a coherent and scaffolded instructional plan. By discussing the scope and sequence of the standards with ChatGPT, teachers can receive recommendations on the logical progression of concepts and skills. This ensures that instruction builds upon previous knowledge and supports students' mastery of the standards over time. For example, a high school history teacher can consult ChatGPT to determine the optimal order in which to teach different historical eras or events.

Additionally, ChatGPT can provide examples and resources that align with specific standards, helping teachers design engaging and targeted lessons. Whether it's suggesting relevant texts for a literature unit or providing authentic data sets for a math lesson, ChatGPT can assist teachers in selecting appropriate materials that support the desired learning outcomes.

Example Prompt/Dialogue:

Teacher: "ChatGPT, I am planning my unit on geometry for my sixth-grade math class. Can you help me access the relevant standards and suggest a sequence for introducing the different geometric concepts?"

ChatGPT: "Certainly! Here are the Common Core State Standards for geometry in sixth grade, and I recommend introducing concepts like lines, angles, and shapes before moving on to more complex topics like area and volume. I can provide you with exemplars, hands-on activities, and online resources aligned with each standard to support your instruction."

By leveraging ChatGPT to access and sequence standards, teachers can ensure their instruction is well-aligned with the desired learning outcomes. This allows for a more coherent and purposeful approach to lesson planning and curriculum design, supporting student progress and achievement.

Clarifying Learning Objectives
After accessing the standards for instruction, teachers are expected to demonstrate their ability to establish and communicate clear learning objectives. ChatGPT can be a valuable tool to help teachers clarify and refine their learning objectives, ensuring they align with the standards and expectations of the curriculum.

Aligning Learning Objectives with Standards:
ChatGPT can assist teachers in aligning their learning objectives with specific standards, such as the Common Core State Standards (CCSS) or the Next Generation Science Standards (NGSS). By engaging in interactive dialogues, teachers can request guidance on how to craft clear and measurable learning objectives that align with the content and skills outlined in the standards.

Example Prompt/Dialogue:

Teacher: "ChatGPT, I teach fourth-grade mathematics, and I'm struggling to align my learning objectives with the CCSS. Can you provide guidance on how to do that effectively?"

ChatGPT: "Certainly! To align your learning objectives with the CCSS in fourth-grade mathematics, you should focus on specific domains and clusters within the standards. For example, you can create learning objectives that target operations and algebraic thinking, number and operations in base ten, or measurement and data. Let's work together to craft learning objectives that align with these domains and clusters."

Example Prompt/Dialogue :

Teacher: "ChatGPT, I'm a high school English Language Arts teacher, and I need help aligning my learning objectives with the ELA standards. Can you provide guidance?"

ChatGPT: "Certainly! To align your learning objectives with the ELA standards, you can consider specific strands, such as reading literature, writing, or language. You can craft learning objectives that focus on analyzing complex texts, writing arguments, or applying language conventions. Let's collaborate to develop learning objectives that align with the ELA standards for your specific grade level."

Refining Learning Objectives for Differentiation:

ChatGPT can support teachers in refining their learning objectives to cater to the diverse needs of their students. By engaging in dialogues with ChatGPT, teachers can explore different ways to scaffold their learning objectives and create opportunities for differentiation within their instruction.

Example Prompt/Dialogue:

Teacher: "ChatGPT, I teach second-grade science, and I want to differentiate my learning objectives to meet the needs of my diverse students. Can you provide some ideas?"

ChatGPT: "Certainly! To differentiate your learning objectives in second-grade science, you can consider offering multiple entry points or pathways for students to demonstrate understanding. For example, you can provide visual aids or manipulatives for hands-on learners, offer extension activities for advanced learners, or provide additional support for struggling learners. Let's discuss specific strategies and modifications you can make to your learning objectives to support differentiation."

Example Prompt/Dialogue:

Teacher: "ChatGPT, I'm a middle school social studies teacher, and I want to ensure my learning objectives are inclusive and address the diverse needs of my students. How can I achieve that?"

ChatGPT: "Certainly! To address the diverse needs of your students in middle school social studies, you can design learning objectives that promote critical thinking and multiple perspectives. You can incorporate cooperative learning activities, provide options for student choice, or integrate multimedia resources to engage different learning styles. Let's explore specific ways to refine your learning objectives to foster inclusivity and address the diverse needs of your students."

By utilizing ChatGPT to clarify and refine their learning objectives, teachers can ensure that their instructional planning aligns with the standards and addresses the diverse needs of their students

Clarifying Lesson Design Components:
ChatGPT can assist teachers in understanding the essential components of effective lesson design. By engaging in interactive dialogues, teachers can ask ChatGPT to break down the requirements outlined in the framework and provide detailed explanations of each component. For example:

Example Prompt/Dialogue:

Teacher: "ChatGPT, I'm a third-grade science teacher, and I want to ensure my lesson plans meet the requirements for effective instructional design. Can you explain the key components I should consider?"

ChatGPT: "Certainly! Effective lesson design in third-grade science typically includes clear learning objectives aligned with the Next Generation Science Standards (NGSS), engaging hands-on activities or experiments, opportunities for students to ask questions and make observations, and assessments that gauge their understanding of the NGSS performance expectations. Let's explore some specific strategies and exemplars that align with these components."

Example Prompt/Dialogue:

Teacher: "ChatGPT, I teach high school mathematics, and I'm seeking clarification on the planning requirements for a complex lesson. Can you help me understand the key components?"

ChatGPT: "Certainly! For a complex high school math lesson, you would want to consider incorporating clear learning objectives aligned with the Common Core State Standards (CCSS), anticipatory sets to engage students, problem-solving tasks that require critical thinking, opportunities for collaborative work, formative assessments, and connections to real-world applications. Let's discuss specific exemplars of complex lesson plans in mathematics that demonstrate these components and align with the CCSS."

Providing Exemplars of Effective Lesson Plans:
ChatGPT can offer examples of well-designed lesson plans to guide teachers in their planning and preparation. These examples showcase the integration of instructional strategies, differentiation techniques, and alignment with standards and learning objectives, including the CCSS and NGSS. By examining these examples, teachers can gain insights into the elements that make a lesson plan effective and see how they can apply those principles to their own instructional practices.

Example Prompt/Dialogue :

Teacher: "ChatGPT, I teach fifth-grade English Language Arts, and I'm looking for exemplars of effective lesson plans for teaching reading comprehension aligned with the CCSS. Can you provide some examples?"

ChatGPT: "Certainly! Here are some exemplars of well-designed lesson plans that focus on teaching reading comprehension skills to fifth-grade students, aligned with the CCSS. These plans include engaging read-alouds, opportunities for discussion and questioning, vocabulary development activities, and guided practice. These exemplars can serve as a reference as you develop your own lesson plans."

Example Prompt/Dialogue :

Teacher: "ChatGPT, I'm a middle school social studies teacher, and I'm searching for exemplars of well-structured lesson plans for teaching about ancient civilizations that align with the CCSS. Can you help me with some examples?"

ChatGPT: "Certainly! Here are some exemplars of well-designed lesson plans that focus on teaching about ancient civilizations in middle school social studies, aligned with the CCSS. These plans incorporate engaging activities, primary and secondary source analysis, discussions on cultural and historical perspectives, and formative assessments. These exemplars can serve as a starting point for your own lesson planning."

Aligning Assessments with Learning Objectives:

ChatGPT can support teachers in aligning their assessments with the learning objectives and standards outlined in the framework, including the CCSS and NGSS and any set of standards accessible on the internet. By discussing their instructional goals and desired outcomes, teachers can seek guidance from ChatGPT on appropriate assessment strategies and methods that effectively measure student progress.

Example Prompt/Dialogue:

Teacher: "ChatGPT, I teach second-grade mathematics, and I want to align my assessments with the CCSS. Can you provide suggestions on how to do that?"

ChatGPT: "Certainly! To align your assessments with the CCSS in second-grade mathematics, you can consider using performance tasks that assess students' ability to apply mathematical concepts, such as solving word problems, representing data, or demonstrating fluency with basic operations. Additionally, you can design short quizzes or exit tickets that target specific CCSS standards. Let's explore some specific assessment ideas and exemplars that align with the CCSS for second-grade mathematics."

Example Prompt/Dialogue:

Teacher: "ChatGPT, I'm a high school science teacher, and I want to ensure my assessments align with the NGSS. Can you provide guidance on how to do that effectively?"

ChatGPT: "Certainly! To align your assessments with the NGSS in high school science, you can design performance-based assessments that require students to apply scientific practices, analyze data, and construct explanations. You can also include open-ended questions that assess students' understanding of the disciplinary core ideas and crosscutting concepts. Let's discuss specific assessment strategies and exemplars that align with the NGSS for high school science."

By using ChatGPT as a resource, teachers can gain a deeper understanding of the planning and preparation requirements outlined in the district and school evaluative criteria. Through interactive dialogues and access to exemplars aligned with standards such as the CCSS and NGSS, teachers can enhance their lesson planning and instructional practices, ensuring they meet the expectations set forth in their evaluations.

Sample ChatGpt Prompts For Planning Protocols

A. Showing you know your Content - and the best pedagogy to teach it!

Example Prompt:

Teacher: "ChatGPT, I want to demonstrate extensive knowledge of the content and pedagogy in *[Subject]* for *[Grade Level]*. How can I continuously improve my practice and build on prerequisites and misconceptions?"

Example Prompt:

Teacher: "ChatGPT, I want to actively build on prerequisites and misconceptions in *[Subject]* for *[Grade Level]* to enhance my instruction. How can I effectively identify and address student misunderstandings?"

B. Showing that you know all about your students!

Example Prompt:

Teacher: "ChatGPT, I want to demonstrate thorough knowledge of my students' backgrounds, skills, and interests in *[Subject]* for *[Grade Level]*. How can I effectively gather this information and use it to plan for individual student learning?"

Example Prompt:

Teacher: "ChatGPT, I want to differentiate my instruction based on the diverse needs of my students in *[Subject]* for *[Grade Level]*. How can I tailor my lessons to address individual student learning?"

C. Demonstrating your ability to set learning outcomes/objectives

Example Prompts/Dialogue:

Teacher: "ChatGPT, I want to set instructional goals that reflect high-level learning related to the curriculum frameworks and standards in *[Subject]* for *[Grade Level]*. How can I ensure that my goals align with the desired learning outcomes?"

Example Prompts/Dialogue:

Teacher: "ChatGPT, I want to adapt instructional goals to the needs of individual students in *[Subject]* for *[Grade Level]*. How can I ensure that my goals are tailored to address their unique learning needs?"

D. Showing you are resourceful as a teacher

Example Prompt:

Teacher: "ChatGPT, I want to demonstrate knowledge of resources for teaching in *[Subject]* for *[Grade Level]*. How can I effectively seek out and utilize resources from professional organizations and the community?"

Example Prompt:

Teacher: "ChatGPT, I want to be aware of resources available for students who need additional support in *[Subject]* for *[Grade Level]*. How can I ensure that I am knowledgeable about the resources within the school, district, and larger community?"

E. Demonstrating you are able to design instruction that is aligned

Example Prompt:

Teacher: "ChatGPT, I want to design instruction that supports my instructional goals, engages students in meaningful learning, and demonstrates evidence of student input in *[Subject]* for *[Grade Level]*. How can I ensure that all elements of my instructional design align with these objectives?"

Example Prompt:

Teacher: "ChatGPT, I want to create a lesson or unit with a clear structure that enhances student understanding in *[Subject]* for *[Grade Level]*. How can I ensure that my instructional materials and activities are highly coherent and organized?"

F. Creating Assessments to measure student learning

Example Prompt:

Teacher: "ChatGPT, I want to design student assessments that are fully aligned with my instructional goals in *[Subject]* for *[Grade Level]*. How can I ensure that my assessments have clear criteria and standards that are understood by students?"

Example Prompt:

Teacher: "ChatGPT, I want my students to actively monitor their own progress in achieving the instructional goals in *[Subject]* for *[Grade Level]*. How can I foster self-assessment and student participation in the development of assessment criteria?"

Strategies For Integrating ChatGPT In Planning Protocols

As teachers, we constantly seek ways to enhance our planning and preparation activities to provide meaningful and effective instruction for our students. The advent of AI technology, such as Chat GPT, presents us with exciting opportunities to access valuable insights, gather information, and engage in productive conversations to support our teaching practice.

In this final section of this episode, we will explore strategies for integrating Chat GPT into our planning and preparation activities. These strategies will empower us to leverage the capabilities of Chat GPT to deepen our content knowledge, analyze standards, sequence and spiral skills, develop learning objectives, plan assessments, gather student information, personalize instruction, identify and utilize resources, and reflect on our practice.

Accessing Content Knowledge: Use Chat GPT to gain a deeper understanding of the content being taught. Ask questions about specific topics, concepts, or theories to receive detailed explanations and relevant examples. Chat GPT can provide additional resources and references to further enhance your knowledge.

Analyzing Standards: Engage in conversations with Chat GPT to analyze and interpret standards, such as the Common Core State Standards (CCSS) or other curriculum frameworks. Seek clarification on specific expectations and explore ways to align instructional goals with the standards.

Sequencing and Spiraling Skills: Collaborate with Chat GPT to design a logical progression of learning that builds upon prior knowledge and spirals skills through the curriculum. Discuss strategies for sequencing standards, identifying prerequisite skills, and incorporating review opportunities to reinforce learning.

Developing Learning Objectives: Utilize Chat GPT to refine and develop clear and measurable learning objectives that align with instructional goals and standards. Seek guidance on incorporating higher-order thinking skills, real-world application, and student engagement into the learning objectives.

Planning Assessments: Engage in dialogue with Chat GPT to design authentic and aligned assessments that accurately measure student learning. Discuss various assessment strategies, such as performance tasks, projects, or formative assessments, and explore ways to involve students in the assessment development process.

Gathering Student Information: Seek advice from Chat GPT on effective methods to gather comprehensive information about students' backgrounds, interests, and learning needs. Explore strategies like surveys, interest inventories, or one-on-one conferences to create a holistic understanding of your students.

Personalizing Instruction: Collaborate with Chat GPT to adapt instruction to meet the diverse needs of your students. Discuss differentiated instructional strategies, accommodations, or modifications based on individual student profiles and learning preferences.

Identifying and Utilizing Resources: Engage in conversations with Chat GPT to identify relevant teaching resources, both within professional organizations and the larger community. Explore ways to leverage digital tools, educational platforms, or community partnerships to enhance instruction and support student learning.

Reflecting on Practice: Use Chat GPT as a reflective tool to analyze and refine your teaching practices. Seek feedback on lesson plans, instructional strategies, or classroom management techniques. Engage in discussions that promote professional growth and continuous improvement.

Engaging in dialogue with Chat GPT can help us gain clarity, access additional resources, and explore new perspectives that enhance our understanding of the curriculum and instructional goals. It can provide us with valuable guidance and ideas to create a learning environment that meets the diverse needs of our students.

However, it is important to remember that while Chat GPT is a powerful tool, our professional judgment and expertise are crucial in adapting its suggestions to fit our unique classroom context and student population. The strategies presented here will serve as a starting point to harness the potential of Chat GPT in our planning and preparation activities, while allowing room for our professional judgment to guide our decisions.

Episode Two
Prompting Paradigm: Classroom Culture and Environment

Exploring The Components of Classroom Culture and Environment

As a teacher it is critical that you focus on creating an optimal learning environment that promotes student engagement, collaboration, and a positive classroom culture. This section emphasizes the teacher's ability to establish a supportive atmosphere where students feel safe, valued, and motivated to learn and strategies to utilize ChatGPT to A.C.E. that evaluation.

Creating such an environment requires teachers to have a deep understanding of the components of a successful classroom culture/environment and how to employ effective instructional strategies to meet this mark and A.C.E. their evaluation in this area. ChatGPT can serve as a valuable tool to assist teachers in navigating the intricacies of their classroom culture and environment to enhance their instructional practices.

Building a Positive Classroom Culture:
ChatGPT can support teachers in fostering a positive classroom culture by providing strategies and resources to establish clear expectations, develop strong relationships with students, and promote a sense of belonging. For instance, a middle school teacher seeking advice on building positive student-teacher relationships can engage with ChatGPT to explore strategies such as interest surveys, one-on-one conferences, or cooperative learning activities that cultivate a positive learning environment.

Promoting Student Engagement:
Engaging students in meaningful learning experiences is a key aspect of effective teaching. ChatGPT can offer a plethora of ideas and instructional strategies to promote student engagement across various grade levels and subjects. Whether it's incorporating hands-on activities, gamification, or technology integration, ChatGPT can provide guidance on innovative approaches to capture students' interest and deepen their understanding.

Effective Classroom Management:

Maintaining a well-managed classroom is essential for creating an environment conducive to learning. ChatGPT can help teachers navigate challenges related to classroom management by offering insights into behavior management techniques, strategies to address disruptions, and methods for establishing clear routines and procedures. By interacting with ChatGPT, teachers can gain additional tools and perspectives to address various classroom scenarios effectively.

Differentiation and Individualization:

Meeting the diverse needs of students is a fundamental aspect of effective teaching. ChatGPT can provide support to teachers in differentiating instruction and individualizing learning experiences. Teachers can engage in dialogue with ChatGPT to explore strategies for accommodating students with varying abilities, adapting materials for diverse learners, and incorporating personalized approaches to instruction.

Collaboration and Community Building:

Creating a sense of community within the classroom and promoting collaboration among students is crucial for fostering a supportive learning environment. ChatGPT can offer ideas and techniques for facilitating cooperative learning activities, promoting peer interactions, and encouraging student collaboration. By leveraging ChatGPT's guidance, teachers can enhance their ability to create a collaborative and inclusive classroom culture.

Example Prompt/Dialogue:

Teacher: "ChatGPT, I want to establish a positive classroom culture in my high school English class. Can you provide me with some strategies to build strong relationships with my students?"

ChatGPT: "Certainly! Here are some strategies you can implement: [provides examples such as icebreaker activities, student-centered discussions, and positive reinforcement techniques]. These strategies have proven to be effective in fostering positive student-teacher relationships in high school settings."

By utilizing ChatGPT as a resource for navigating the components of classroom culture and environment - teachers can gain valuable insights, access instructional strategies, and discover new approaches to create a positive and productive classroom environment. ChatGPT empowers teachers to develop instructional practices that promote student engagement, build a supportive community, and lay the foundation for meaningful learning experiences.

Remember, ChatGPT is here to support your professional growth by providing personalized guidance, resources, and adaptable strategies. By leveraging ChatGPT's capabilities, teachers can cultivate an optimal learning environment that enhances student motivation, collaboration, and overall academic success in K-12 education.

Decoding The Indicators And Desired Outcomes

In this section we will highlight the elements that create a positive and conducive learning environment where students feel safe, engaged, and supported. This section emphasizes the teacher's role in establishing and maintaining an environment that promotes respectful and inclusive interactions, establishes clear expectations, and supports the social-emotional well-being of students and how ChatGPT can aide you in meeting this mark to A.C.E. your evaluation.

We will delve into each several key areas you and ChatGPT will want to focus upon, examining their significance and exploring strategies for effectively addressing them. By understanding and implementing these components teachers can create a classroom environment that fosters collaboration, builds relationships, and enhances student learning.

A. Respectful Classroom Environment and Rapport Building: This component focuses on the teacher's efforts to build positive relationships with students and foster an atmosphere of mutual respect. It involves establishing clear expectations, promoting inclusivity, and nurturing a sense of belonging.

B. Setting the Tone for a Learning Culture Classroom: This component emphasizes the teacher's role in creating a culture that values learning and encourages student engagement. It involves setting high expectations, promoting a growth mindset, and fostering a supportive and collaborative learning community.

C. Making Sure you Have Tight Systems, Structure and Procedures: This component addresses the teacher's ability to establish and maintain effective classroom routines and procedures. It involves organizing the physical space., managing transitions, and ensuring smooth and efficient operation of classroom activities.

D. Promoting High Standards of Behavior: This component focuses on the teacher's skill in maintaining a positive and productive classroom climate through proactive behavior management strategies. It involves establishing clear behavior expectations, implementing appropriate consequences, and promoting self-regulation skills.

E. Best Practices in Arranging and Organizing the Classroom: This component examines the teacher's ability to design and arrange the physical space. to support instructional goals, student engagement, and collaboration. It involves creating an environment that is safe, accessible, and conducive to learning.

As we explore each component, we will discuss strategies, examples, and practical tips to help teachers create a positive and supportive classroom environment. Remember, these components are interconnected, and effective implementation of one component often influences the others. By focusing on these components, teachers can cultivate an environment that promotes student well-being, encourages active participation, and facilitates optimal learning experiences.

Let's now dive into each component and explore ways to create a vibrant and nurturing classroom environment that supports student growth and success.

Leveraging Chat GPT To Foster A Positive Classroom Environment

A. Respectful Classroom Environment and Rapport Building
Creating an environment of respect and rapport is fundamental to fostering positive relationships with students. When students feel valued, supported, and understood, they are more likely to engage in meaningful learning experiences. Here are some strategies to cultivate a respectful and rapport-building classroom environment:

Establish Clear Expectations: Collaborate with students to develop a set of class norms and expectations that promote respect, inclusivity, and active participation. Discuss the importance of treating one another with kindness and empathy.

Example Prompt:

Teacher: "Chat GPT, how can I involve my students in creating class norms and expectations that foster respect and rapport?

> ***Example Prompt:***
>
> **Teacher:** "ChatGPT, What are some effective ways to discuss the importance of empathy and kindness with my students?"

Build Positive Relationships: Take time to get to know your students as individuals, showing genuine interest in their lives, interests, and backgrounds. Incorporate activities that encourage students to share about themselves and create opportunities for positive interactions among peers.

> ***Example Prompt:***
>
> **Teacher:** "ChatGPT, what are some strategies to build positive relationships with my students?"

> ***Example Prompt:***
>
> **Teacher:** "ChatGPT, can you suggest activities or icebreakers that can help foster a sense of belonging and connectedness in the classroom?"

Promote Inclusivity and Diversity: Create a classroom environment that celebrates diversity and promotes inclusivity. Incorporate culturally responsive teaching practices, diverse literature, and resources that reflect the backgrounds and experiences of your students.

> ***Example Prompt:***
>
> **Teacher:** "ChatGPT, how can I ensure that my classroom materials and resources are inclusive and representative of all my students?"

> ***Example Prompt:***
>
> **Teacher:** "ChatGPT, are there specific strategies I can use to foster a sense of inclusivity among my students?

Foster Open Communication: Create a safe and supportive space for students to express their thoughts, opinions, and concerns. Encourage active listening and model respectful communication. Address conflicts or misunderstandings promptly and constructively.

Example Prompt:

Teacher: "ChatGPT, what are some effective strategies for promoting open communication in the classroom?

Example Prompt:

Teacher: "ChatGPT, how can I encourage my students to share their thoughts and perspectives during class discussions?

Remember, building a respectful and rapport-building environment takes time and ongoing effort. By consistently demonstrating respect, actively listening to students, and fostering positive relationships, you create a classroom environment where students feel valued and empowered to engage in their learning journey.

B. Setting the Tone for a Learning Culture Classroom

Next, we will explore the second component which is setting the tone for a Learning Culture classroom. Establishing such a culture for learning sets the tone for student engagement, motivation, and academic growth. It involves creating an environment where students are encouraged to take risks, collaborate, and actively participate in their own learning. Here are strategies to foster a culture for learning:

Set High Expectations: Communicate clear and ambitious academic expectations for all students. Encourage students to strive for excellence, set goals, and take ownership of their learning.

Example Prompt:

Teacher: "ChatGPT, how can I effectively communicate high expectations to my students?"

Example Prompt:

Teacher: "ChatGPT, can you suggest strategies for motivating students to set ambitious goals?"

Foster a Growth Mindset: Help students develop a growth mindset by emphasizing the value of effort, resilience, and learning from mistakes. Encourage them to embrA.C.E. challenges, persevere, and believe in their ability to grow and improve.

Example Prompt:

Teacher: "ChatGPT, what are some ways to promote a growth mindset in my classroom?

Example Prompt:

Teacher: "ChatGPT, Can you provide examples of how I can encourage students to embrA.C.E. challenges and view mistakes as learning opportunities?"

Create a Supportive Learning Community: Establish a classroom culture that values collaboration, teamwork, and mutual support. Encourage students to work together, share ideas, and learn from one another.

Example Prompt:

Teacher: "ChatGPT, how can I foster a collaborative learning community in my classroom?

Example Prompt:

Teacher: "ChatGPT, are there specific strategies or activities that promote teamwork and peer learning?

Provide Meaningful and Relevant Learning Experiences: Design instructional activities that connect to students' interests, prior knowledge, and real-world contexts. Engage students in hands-on experiences, problem-solving tasks, and inquiry-based learning.

Example Prompt:

Teacher: "ChatGPT, what are some ways to make learning more meaningful and relevant for my students?

> **Example Prompt:**
>
> **Teacher:** "ChatGPT, can you suggest examples of hands-on activities or projects that promote active engagement?

By establishing a culture for learning, you create an environment where students are motivated, actively involved, and excited about their educational journey. Remember to adapt these strategies to suit the grade level, subject area, and specific needs of your students.

C: Making Sure you Have Tight Systems, Structure and Procedures:
Effective management of classroom procedures contributes to a well-organized and efficient learning environment. It involves establishing clear routines, managing transitions, and ensuring smooth classroom operations. Here are strategies to support effective classroom procedure management:

Establish Clear Routines: Set clear expectations for daily routines and procedures, such as entering and exiting the classroom, transitioning between activities, and accessing materials. Teach and practice these routines with students to ensure understanding and consistency.

> **Example Prompt:**
>
> **Teacher:** "ChatGPT, what are some effective strategies for establishing clear routines in the classroom?

> **Example Prompt:**
>
> **Teacher:** "Can you provide examples of how I can teach and reinforce classroom procedures to my students?

Manage Transitions: Smooth transitions between activities help maximize instructional time and minimize disruptions. Implement strategies such as visual cues, timers, or transition signals to facilitate smooth transitions and keep students engaged.

> *Example Prompt:*
>
> **Teacher:** "ChatGPT, how can I effectively manage transitions between activities in my classroom?"

> *Example Prompt:*
>
> **Teacher:** "ChatGPT, can you suggest specific techniques or tools that can help improve transition times?"

Organize Materials and Resources: Designate specific areas for materials, supplies, and resources, ensuring easy access for students. Teach students how to independently locate and return materials, promoting responsibility and organization.

> *Example Prompt:*
>
> **Teacher:** "ChatGPT, what are some effective ways to organize classroom materials and resources?

> *Example Prompt:*
>
> **Teacher:** "ChatGPT, how can I teach my students to independently manage and locate materials?

Implement Behavior Management Strategies: Proactively address behavior expectations by establishing clear behavior guidelines, rules, and consequences. Use positive reinforcement, praise, and rewards to encourage desired behaviors and create a positive classroom climate.

> *Example Prompt:*
>
> **Teacher:** "ChatGPT, what are some effective behavior management strategies I can implement in my classroom?"

Example Prompt:

Teacher: "ChatGPT, can you provide examples of how I can reinforce positive behaviors and address challenging behaviors?"

By effectively managing classroom procedures, you create a structured and well-run learning environment that supports student engagement, reduces disruptions, and maximizes learning opportunities. Remember to adapt these strategies to fit the unique needs and age level of your students.

D. Promoting High Standards of Behavior

Managing student behavior is an essential component of creating a conducive learning environment. It involves establishing clear behavior expectations, promoting positive behavior, and addressing challenging behaviors effectively. Here are strategies to support effective management of student behavior:

Establish Clear Behavior Expectations: Communicate clear behavior expectations and rules to students. Involve them in the process by collaboratively creating classroom norms that promote respect, responsibility, and positive interactions.

Example Prompt:

Teacher: "ChatGPT, how can I establish clear behavior expectations in my classroom?"

Example Prompt:

Teacher: "ChatGPT, can you provide examples of how I can involve students in creating behavior norms?"

Promote Positive Behavior: Encourage and reinforce positive behavior by using a variety of strategies such as praise, recognition, and rewards. Create a positive classroom culture where students feel valued and motivated to demonstrate appropriate behavior.

Example Prompt:

Teacher: "ChatGPT, what are some effective ways to promote positive behavior in the classroom?

Example Prompt:

Teacher: "ChatGPT, can you suggest specific techniques or activities that can foster a positive classroom culture?

Address Challenging Behaviors: Develop a proactive approach to address challenging behaviors by identifying potential triggers and implementing appropriate interventions. Utilize strategies such as individual behavior plans, restorative practices, and differentiated instruction to support students with diverse needs.

Example Prompt:

Teacher: "ChatGPT, how can I effectively address challenging behaviors in my classroom?"

Example Prompt:

Teacher: "ChatGPT, can you provide examples of strategies to support students with specific behavior challenges?"

Foster a Supportive Classroom Community: Create a classroom environment that promotes empathy, understanding, and social-emotional development. Implement activities and discussions that encourage cooperation, conflict resolution, and self-regulation skills.

Example Prompt:

Teacher: "ChatGPT, what are some strategies to foster a supportive classroom community?"

Example Prompt:

Teacher: "ChatGPT, Can you suggest activities or resources that promote social-emotional development?"

By effectively managing student behavior, you establish a positive and respectful learning environment where students feel safe, engaged, and empowered. Remember to adapt these strategies to meet the unique needs and circumstances of your students.

E: Best Practices in Arranging and Organizing the Classroom:
The physical layout of the classroom plays a crucial role in creating an environment that supports learning, collaboration, and student engagement. Organizing the physical space. involves intentional arrangement of furniture, materials, and resources to optimize student interaction and instructional activities. Here are strategies to effectively organize the physical space.:

Consider Classroom Layout: Determine the most suitable classroom layout based on instructional needs and student interactions. Options may include traditional rows, clusters, or flexible seating arrangements that allow for collaboration and movement.

Example Prompt:

Teacher: "ChatGPT, what are some considerations when determining the classroom layout?"

Example Prompt:

Teacher: "ChatGPT, Can you provide examples of different seating arrangements and their benefits?"

Maximize Accessibility: Arrange furniture, supplies, and materials in a way that ensures easy accessibility for all students. Consider students with physical disabilities, visual impairments, or diverse learning needs to create an inclusive environment.

Example Prompt:

Teacher: "ChatGPT, How can I maximize accessibility in my classroom design?"

Example Prompt:

Teacher: "ChatGPT, can you suggest strategies or modifications to support students with different needs?

Create Functional Learning Areas: Designate specific areas within the classroom to serve different purposes, such as a reading corner, collaborative workstations, or a maker space. Clearly label and organize materials and resources in these areas.

Example Prompt:

Teacher: "ChatGPT, what are some ideas for creating functional learning areas in the classroom?"

Example Prompt:

Teacher: "ChatGPT, can you provide examples of how I can organize materials in these designated areas?"

Utilize Wall Space: Make use of wall space to display anchor charts, student work, visual aids, and other educational resources. Ensure that materials are relevant, visible, and accessible to support student learning and reference.

Example Prompt:

Teacher: "ChatGPT, how can I effectively utilize wall space in my classroom?"

Example Prompt:

Teacher: "ChatGPT, can you suggest ideas for displaying student work or creating interactive wall displays?"

By organizing the physical space. in your classroom, you create an environment that enhances student learning, collaboration, and engagement. Remember to adapt these strategies to accommodate the unique needs, grade level, and subject area of your classroom.

Interactive Dialogue With Chatgpt For Addressing Classroom Environment Challenges

In this section, we delve into the practical implementation of ChatGPT as a valuable tool for teachers in addressing classroom environment challenges **in real-time.** By keeping chat streams open on their computers, teachers can engage in interactive dialogue with ChatGPT and brainstorm quick and effective solutions to common issues that arise throughout the day. This episode focuses on how teachers can leverage ChatGPT to foster a positive and conducive learning atmosphere, taking into account various grade levels, types of classes, and unique **challenges** that may emerge.

Challenge 1: Building Rapport with Students

Amidst the demands of a busy day, teachers can turn to ChatGPT for immediate strategies to build rapport with their students. By engaging in real-time dialogue, teachers can seek advice on ice-breaker activities, personalized interactions, and ways to connect with students on a deeper level. Prompts may include:

Example Prompt:

Teacher: "ChatGPT, how can I effectively build rapport with elementary students, particularly during the initial weeks of school?"

Example Prompt:

Teacher: "ChatGPT, what are some engaging ice-breaker activities suitable for a grade 6 class?"

Example Prompt:

Teacher: "How can I personalize my interactions with high school students to foster a sense of rapport?"

Challenge 2: Promoting Inclusion and Diversity

Teachers often encounter challenges related to promoting inclusion and celebrating diversity in the classroom. ChatGPT can provide prompt ideas, discussion topics, and resources to create an inclusive environment. Teachers can ask for suggestions tailored to their specific context, such as:

Example Prompt:

Teacher: "ChatGPT, what are some effective strategies for creating an inclusive environment that respects and values the diverse backgrounds and cultures of my students?"

Example Prompt:

Teacher: "ChatGPT, how can I incorporate diverse perspectives in a middle school social studies lesson?"

Example Prompt:

Teacher: "What are some strategies for fostering inclusion in a kindergarten classroom?"

Challenge 3: Managing Classroom Behavior

Teachers frequently face unexpected behavior challenges that require immediate attention. ChatGPT can offer on-the-spot strategies, such as redirection techniques, positive reinforcement ideas, and quick interventions to address disruptive behavior and maintain a positive classroom atmosphere. While you always want to follow your school/district's policies and procedures, teachers can seek guidance for specific non-serious classroom scenarios, such as:

Example Prompt:

Teacher: "ChatGPT, what are some proactive approaches I can employ to manage behavior and promote a positive learning environment in my elementary classroom?"

> **Example Prompt:**
>
> **Teacher:** "ChatGPT, what are some effective methods of positive reinforcement that I can utilize to foster a positive classroom climate and motivate my students?"

> **Example Prompt:**
>
> **Teacher:** "ChatGPT, how can I address challenging behaviors and maintain a positive classroom atmosphere in my middle or high school class?"

> **Example Prompt:**
>
> **Teacher:** "What are some strategies to de-escalate conflicts between students in an elementary school setting?"

Challenge 4: Encouraging Collaborative Learning

Promoting collaboration among students is essential for a productive learning environment. ChatGPT can provide teachers with real-time suggestions and activities to encourage collaborative learning. Teachers can ask for grade-appropriate ideas, such as:

> **Example Prompt:**
>
> **Teacher:** "ChatGPT, what are some cooperative learning strategies suitable for a third-grade math class?"

> **Example Prompt:**
>
> **Teacher:** "How can I encourage active participation and collaboration during a group project in a middle school English class?"

> **Example Prompt:**
>
> **Teacher:** "ChatGPT, how can I create a collaborative learning environment in online classes where students can actively engage and interact with their peers?"

Challenge 5: Promoting Emotional Well-being

Promoting Emotional Well-being is crucial for fostering a supportive classroom environment. Explore these challenge prompts to ensure students' emotional needs are addressed, enhancing their overall well-being and learning outcomes.

Example Prompt:

Teacher: "ChatGPT, what are some strategies I can implement to support the emotional well-being of my elementary students, especially during challenging times?"

Example Prompt:

Teacher: "ChatGPT, how can I address the emotional needs of my adolescent students and create a safe space for them to express themselves?"

Example Prompt:

Teacher: "ChatGPT, what are some age-appropriate activities or discussions I can implement in my classroom to promote emotional well-being among my students?"

Example Prompt:

Teacher: "ChatGPT, can you provide me with strategies to create a safe and supportive environment that encourages emotional expression and empathy in young learners?"

Example Prompt:

Teacher: "ChatGPT, how can I address and support students who may be experiencing emotional difficulties using ChatGPT as a resource?"

Example Prompt:

Teacher: "ChatGPT, how can I use ChatGPT to address and provide guidance on issues such as bullying, peer pressure, and emotional challenges among my students?"

Example Prompt:

Teacher: "ChatGPT, what strategies or topics can I explore with ChatGPT to facilitate discussions on mental health, stress management, and self-care in a high school setting?"

Example Prompt:

Teacher: "ChatGPT, can you provide me with guidance on incorporating mindfulness practices and self-reflection exercises using ChatGPT to support my students' emotional well-being?"

By engaging in interactive dialogue with ChatGPT, teachers can quickly access a wealth of ideas and strategies to address classroom environment challenges. Whether it's building rapport with students, promoting inclusion, managing behavior, or fostering collaboration, ChatGPT serves as a valuable resource for teachers seeking real-time solutions.

Best Proactive Practices For Utilizing ChatGPT In Creating An Optimal Learning Environment

As teachers strive to excel on their evaluations, there are several actions they can **proactively** take themselves to leverage ChatGPT and create an optimal learning environment. Here are some practical steps teachers can implement, along with corresponding prompts to support their efforts:

Cultivate Respectful Classroom Interactions:
Action: Foster a positive and respectful classroom environment by modeling genuine warmth and care.

Example Prompt:

Teacher: "ChatGPT, how can I greet each student individually at the beginning of the class to establish a welcoming atmosphere?"

Foster a Culture of Excellence and Student Ownership:

Action: Empower students to take pride in their work and drive improvements in their learning journey.

Example Prompt:

Teacher: "How can you encourage students to initiate revisions or enhancements to their projects? Provide them with prompts that inspire them to raise the bar."

Demonstrate a Passionate Commitment to the Subject:

Action: Showcase your enthusiasm for the subject matter to ignite student interest and engagement.

Example Prompt:

Teacher: "ChatGPT, how can I use ChatGPT to pose thought-provoking questions or present real-world applications that spark students' curiosity and passion for the topic?"

Establish Seamless Classroom Routines and Procedures:

Action: Streamline classroom routines and involve students in their smooth operation.

Example Prompt:

Teacher: "ChatGPT, how can I collaborate with ChatGPT to reinforce daily procedures, such as submitting assignments, requesting permission to speak, or organizing materials?"

Encourage Appropriate Student Behavior and Engagement:
Action: Engage students in setting behavior expectations and monitoring their own conduct.

Example Prompt:

Teacher: "Chat GPT, how can I involve students in establishing class norms and encouraging mutual respect, using ChatGPT to facilitate a discussion on expected behaviors?"

Implement Subtle and Preventive Behavior Management:
Action: Utilize ChatGPT to proactively monitor student behavior and tailor responses accordingly.

Example Prompt:

Teacher: "ChatGPT, How can I leverage ChatGPT to identify potential disruptions and intervene early on, providing individualized support to address specific student needs?"

By taking these proactive steps and utilizing the prompts provided, teachers can effectively harness the power of ChatGPT to address classroom environment challenges, promote student ownership

Episode Three
<u>Impressive and Innovative Instructional Prompts</u>

Overview of The Components of I&I Instruction

Impressive and Innovative Instruction consists of five essential components: *a) Communicating Consciously b) Crafting Questions and Classroom Discourse, c) Are Students Engaged? d) Feedback for Improved Student Performance, and e) Instructional Pivots in Response to Emerging Student Needs.* Let's explore each component and discover how teachers can utilize ChatGPT to enhance their instructional practices.

A. *Communicating Consciously:*

This element emphasizes the teacher's aptitude to effectively communicate information, guaranteeing both clarity and accuracy. It encompasses using exact terminology, presenting unambiguous directions, and adjusting communication to cater to the requirements of a diverse group of students.

B. *Crafting Questions and Classroom Discourse:*

This component emphasizes the teacher's skill in utilizing effective questioning techniques to promote critical thinking and meaningful discussions. It involves asking thought-provoking questions, facilitating student-led discussions, and encouraging active participation.

C. *Are Students Engaged?:*

This component addresses the teacher's ability to actively engage students in the learning process. It involves employing various instructional strategies, incorporating technology, and providing opportunities for hands-on learning and collaboration.

D. *Feedback for Improved Student Performance:*

This component focuses on the teacher's role in providing constructive feedback to support student growth and improvement. It involves offering specific and actionable feedback, promoting self-assessment, and using various feedback formats, such as written comments or verbal discussions.

E. *Instructional Pivots and Responding to Emerging Student Needs:*

This component examines the teacher's adaptability and responsiveness to meet the diverse needs of students. It involves adjusting instructional strategies based on student feedback, differentiating instruction, and making timely modifications to lesson plans.

As we delve into each of these components, we will provide practical examples, prompts, and ChatGPT sample responses to demonstrate how teachers can leverage technology to enhance their instructional practices. Remember, these components are interconnected, and effective implementation of one component can positively impact the others. By focusing on these components, teachers can foster an optimal learning environment, promote student engagement, and facilitate meaningful learning experiences.

By utilizing ChatGPT and considering the prompts provided, teachers can enhance their instructional practices in communicating clearly, using effective questioning techniques, engaging students, providing valuable feedback, and demonstrating flexibility and responsiveness to emerging student needs.. This collaboration with ChatGPT can support teachers in creating an optimal learning environment and promoting student success.

Now, let's explore each component and discover the ways in which ChatGPT can support teachers in their instructional endeavors.

Analyzing The Indicators And Instructional Techniques

A. *Communicating Consciously:*
To excel in the component of "Communicating Consciously" within this area, it is crucial for teachers to exhibit exemplary practices in their oral and written communication. This involves clear and expressive communication that anticipates possible student misconceptions. By employing ChatGPT as a tool for analysis, teachers can further enhance their understanding and refine their instructional techniques. Here are some prompts to assist teachers in analyzing their practices:

Example Prompt/Dialogue:

Teacher: "ChatGPT, how can I ensure clarity in my oral and written communication?"

ChatGPT: ""To ensure clarity in your communication, you can:
- Use precise language and avoid jargon.
- Provide explicit instructions and explanations.
- Break down complex concepts into simpler terms.
- Offer real-life examples or visual aids to support understanding."

Example Prompt/Dialogue:

Teacher: "ChatGPT, how can I anticipate and address possible student misconceptions in my communication?

ChatGPT: "To anticipate and address student misconceptions, you can:
- Reflect on common misconceptions related to the topic.
- Incorporate anticipatory questions that challenge existing misconceptions.
- Provide alternative explanations or multiple perspectives.
- Encourage students to ask questions and clarify any misunderstandings."

Example Prompt/Dialogue:

Teacher: "ChatGPT, How can I tailor my communication to meet the diverse needs of my students?"

ChatGPT: "To meet the diverse needs of your students, you can:
- Adapt your language and communication style to accommodate different language proficiency levels.
- Provide additional support or scaffolding for students who require it.
- Offer opportunities for students to share their understanding in various formats (e.g., verbal, written, visual).
- Consider cultural differences and backgrounds when conveying information."

Example Prompt/Dialogue:

Teacher: "ChatGPT, how can I leverage technology to enhance my communication with students?

ChatGPT: "To leverage technology in your communication, you can:
- Utilize online platforms or learning management systems to provide written instructions or resources.
- Incorporate multimedia elements (e.g., videos, interactive presentations) to enhance understanding.
- Utilize digital tools for real-time feedback and clarification.
- Encourage online discussions or collaborative platforms for students to share their thoughts and questions."

By engaging in a reflective dialogue with ChatGPT, teachers can gain valuable insights into their instructional techniques and identify areas for improvement. Remember to consider the specific grade levels, content areas, and unique challenges within your classroom when using these prompts. The aim is to refine your communication skills, anticipate student misconceptions, and foster a learning environment where clarity and expression are paramount.

B. *Crafting Questions and Classroom Discourse*

In the component of "Crafting Questions and Classroom Discourse" teachers strive for excellence by fostering student engagement and active participation in discussions through thoughtful question crafting and facilitating inclusive discourse. When utilizing ChatGPT to analyze their practices, teachers can gain valuable insights to further refine their instructional techniques. Here are prompts that can assist teachers in analyzing their approaches:

Example Prompt/Dialogue:

Teacher: "ChatGPT, how can I encourage students to formulate high-level questions?

ChatGPT: "To encourage students to formulate high-level questions, you can:
- Model and provide examples of high-level questions.
- Offer open-ended prompts that stimulate critical thinking and require analysis.
- Create a safe and supportive environment where students feel comfortable asking challenging questions.
- Provide scaffolding or guiding prompts to support students in developing their questions."

Example Prompt/Dialogue:

Teacher: "ChatGPT, how can I ensure all students actively participate in classroom discussions?"

ChatGPT: "To ensure active participation in classroom discussions, you can:
- Establish norms and expectations that promote inclusive participation.
- Use strategies like think-pair-share or small-group discussions to increase engagement.
- Encourage and value diverse perspectives by explicitly acknowledging and incorporating them into the conversation.
- Provide wait time to allow students to process and contribute their thoughts."

Example Prompt/Dialogue:

Teacher: "ChatGPT, how can I facilitate student responsibility for the participation of all students in the discussion?"

ChatGPT: "To facilitate student responsibility for inclusive participation, you can:
- Assign roles or responsibilities within the discussion (e.g., facilitator, recorder) to distribute engagement.
- Implement protocols that ensure equitable speaking opportunities for all students.
- Teach and model active listening skills, such as paraphrasing and building on others' ideas.
- Foster a classroom culture that values and appreciates diverse contributions."

Example Prompt/Dialogue:

Teacher: "How can I leverage technology to enhance question crafting and classroom discourse?"

ChatGPT: ""To leverage technology in question crafting and classroom discourse, you can:
- Utilize digital tools or online platforms that facilitate asynchronous discussions or allow for anonymous contributions.
- Incorporate multimedia resources or online articles to stimulate discussion and generate questions.
- Implement polling or survey tools to gather student responses and opinions.
- Utilize chat or discussion features within virtual learning environments to promote engagement."

By engaging in a reflective dialogue with ChatGPT, teachers can gain insights into their instructional techniques for crafting questions and facilitating classroom discourse. Remember to consider the unique grade levels, content areas, and individual needs of your students as you use these prompts. The goal is to foster an environment where students actively participate, formulate high-level questions, and assume responsibility for inclusive discussions.

C. Are Students Engaged?

In the component of "Are Students Engaged?, teachers strive for high levels of student engagement and active involvement in the learning process. By using ChatGPT to analyze their practices, teachers can gain valuable insights into enhancing student engagement. Here are prompts to help teachers further analyze their instructional techniques:

Example Prompt/Dialogue:

Teacher: "ChatGPT, how can I promote student engagement throughout the lesson?"

ChatGPT: "To promote student engagement throughout the lesson, you can:
- Use hands-on activities, experiments, or simulations that actively involve students in the learning process.
- Incorporate technology tools or multimedia resources to make the content more interactive and engaging.
- Provide opportunities for student choice and autonomy, such as project-based learning or inquiry-based activities.
- Connect the lesson to real-world examples and student interests to increase relevance and engagement."

Example Prompt/Dialogue:

Teacher: "ChatGPT, How can I encourage students to make material contributions to the representation of content, activities, and materials?"

ChatGPT: "To encourage students to make material contributions, you can:
- Implement collaborative learning strategies, such as group projects or discussions, where students contribute their ideas and perspectives.
- Allow students to co-create learning materials, such as visual representations, concept maps, or digital presentations.
- Provide opportunities for student-led discussions or presentations where they share their knowledge and insights.
- Incorporate student voice and choice in decision-making processes related to content selection or learning activities."

Example Prompt/Dialogue:

Teacher: "ChatGPT, how can I structure and pace. the lesson to allow for student reflection and closure?

ChatGPT: ""To structure and pace the lesson for student reflection and closure, you can:
- Allocate dedicated time for students to reflect on their learning, either individually or through group discussions.
- Incorporate summarization activities where students consolidate their understanding and articulate key takeaways.
- Provide opportunities for students to ask questions, seek clarification, or express their thoughts before concluding the lesson.
- Offer closure activities, such as exit tickets or journaling, to facilitate students' reflection on their learning journey."

Example Prompt/Dialogue:

Teacher: "ChatGPT, how can I leverage technology to enhance student engagement and reflection?

ChatGPT: ""To leverage technology in enhancing student engagement and reflection, you can:
- Use interactive online platforms, gamified applications, or virtual reality tools to create immersive learning experiences.
- Integrate multimedia resources, such as videos, animations, or interactive simulations, to engage students visually and kinesthetically.
- Utilize digital assessment tools that provide immediate feedback and allow students to self-reflect on their progress.
- Facilitate online discussions or forums where students can share their thoughts, insights, and reflections."

By engaging in a reflective dialogue with ChatGPT, teachers can gain insights into their instructional techniques for promoting student engagement, facilitating student contributions, and structuring lessons for reflection and closure. Consider the specific grade levels, content areas, and student characteristics as you utilize these prompts to enhance student engagement in your classroom.

D. *Feedback for Improved Student Performance:*

In the component of "Feedback for Improved Student Performance", teachers focus on providing timely and high-quality feedback to students, which students then use to enhance their learning. By leveraging ChatGPT, teachers can further analyze their feedback practices and explore strategies to improve student performance. Here are prompts to support this analysis:

Example Prompt/Dialogue:

Teacher: "ChatGPT, how can I ensure that my feedback to students is timely and consistently of high quality?"

ChatGPT: ""To ensure timely and high-quality feedback, you can:
- Establish clear expectations and criteria for student work, enabling you to provide specific and constructive feedback.
- Implement efficient feedback systems, such as using technology tools for automated grading or providing written comments promptly.
- Offer both formative and summative feedback throughout the learning process, allowing students to make immediate improvements.
- Provide actionable feedback that highlights strengths, identifies areas for growth, and offers suggestions for improvement."

Example Prompt/Dialogue:

Teacher: "ChatGPT, how can I encourage students to make use of the feedback in their learning?"

ChatGPT: "To encourage students to make use of feedback, you can:
- Facilitate feedback discussions or conferences where students have the opportunity to reflect on their work and discuss the feedback received.
- Incorporate self-assessment and peer feedback activities, enabling students to actively engage with feedback and take ownership of their learning.
- Scaffold the process of incorporating feedback by providing guidance on how to interpret and apply feedback to future assignments.
- Monitor student progress and provide ongoing support, ensuring that students understand how to use the feedback effectively."

Example Prompt/Dialogue:

Teacher: "ChatGPT, how can I leverage technology to enhance feedback practices and student performance?"

ChatGPT: "To leverage technology for feedback and improved student performance, you can:
- Utilize online platforms or learning management systems that enable efficient feedback delivery and facilitate student access to feedback.
- Incorporate multimedia feedback, such as video or audio recordings, to provide more detailed explanations or demonstrations.
- Use digital tools that offer interactive feedback features, allowing students to engage with feedback and track their progress over time.
- Provide opportunities for students to submit digital artifacts or portfolios, enabling ongoing feedback and reflection on growth."

Example Prompt/Dialogue:

Teacher: "ChatGPT, how can I promote a growth mindset through my feedback practices?

ChatGPT: "To promote a growth mindset through feedback, you can:
- Emphasize effort, improvement, and the learning process rather than solely focusing on grades or final outcomes.
- Encourage students to view feedback as an opportunity for growth and development, emphasizing that mistakes are valuable for learning.
- Provide specific and actionable feedback that guides students on how to make progress and develop their skills.
- Celebrate and recognize student efforts and progress, fostering a positive and supportive learning environment."

By engaging in reflective dialogue with ChatGPT, teachers can analyze their feedback practices and explore ways to provide timely and high-quality feedback that supports student learning and growth. Consider the unique needs and characteristics of your students as you utilize these prompts to enhance your feedback practices for improved student performance.

E. *Instructional Pivots and Responding to Emerging Student Needs:*

In the component of "Instructional Pivots and Responding to Emerging Student Needs", teachers demonstrate a high level of responsiveness to students' interests, questions, and individual needs. They make necessary adjustments to their lessons and persist in ensuring the success of all students. By leveraging ChatGPT, teachers can further analyze their instructional approaches and explore strategies to effectively respond to emerging student needs. Here are prompts to support this analysis:

Example Prompt/Dialogue:

Teacher: "ChatGPT, how can I be more responsive to students' interests and questions during instruction?"

ChatGPT: "To be more responsive to students' interests and questions, you can:
- Incorporate student choice and inquiry-based activities that allow students to explore topics of interest within the curriculum.
- Encourage students to generate questions and facilitate class discussions where their questions can be explored and answered.
- Use technology tools or online platforms that enable real-time interaction and feedback, fostering engagement and addressing student queries.
- Regularly seek student feedback and input to understand their interests and adjust instruction accordingly."

Example Prompt/Dialogue:

Teacher: "ChatGPT, how can I effectively adjust my lessons when necessary to meet the emerging needs of students?"

ChatGPT: "To effectively adjust your lessons to meet emerging student needs, you can:
- Monitor student progress and understanding through formative assessments, and use the data to identify areas where additional support or modification is needed.
- Differentiate instruction by providing alternative learning resources, activities, or assignments that cater to varying levels of readiness, interests, or learning styles.
- Collaborate with colleagues or utilize professional learning communities to gather insights and share strategies for adapting instruction based on student needs.
- Continuously reflect on student feedback and performance to inform instructional decisions and make timely adjustments."

Example Prompt/Dialogue:

Teacher: "ChatGPT, how can I persist in ensuring the success of all students despite challenges or setbacks?"

ChatGPT: "To persist in ensuring the success of all students, you can:
- Adopt a growth mindset and foster a classroom culture that values effort, resilience, and a belief in the potential of every student to succeed.
- Provide differentiated support and interventions to address individual student needs, whether through additional resources, one-on-one instruction, or small group activities.
- Establish a supportive network of educators, counselors, or specialists who can provide guidance and collaborate in developing strategies to support students facing challenges.
- Implement ongoing progress monitoring to track student growth and adjust instructional approaches as needed."

Example Prompt/Dialogue:

Teacher: "ChatGPT, how can technology tools or resources help me respond to emerging student needs effectively?

ChatGPT: "Technology tools and resources can assist in responding to emerging student needs effectively by:
- Providing access to digital content, online tutorials, or interactive simulations that cater to diverse learning needs and interests.
- Facilitating communication and collaboration among students and teachers, allowing for immediate feedback and support.
- Offering adaptive learning platforms that adjust content and activities based on individual student performance, providing personalized learning experiences.
- Utilizing data analytics and learning management systems to track student progress and identify areas of intervention or additional support."

By engaging in reflective dialogue with ChatGPT, teachers can analyze their instructional pivots and approaches to responding to emerging student needs. Consider the unique characteristics and needs of your students as you utilize these prompts to enhance your responsiveness and ensure the success of all students in your classroom.

As we wrap up the section on Analyzing The Indicators And Instructional Techniques, we have explored the essential elements that contribute to effective teaching practices. From Communicating Consciously to Crafting Questions and Classroom Discourse, Engaging Students, Providing Feedback, and Instructional Pivots, we have delved into the key components that shape instructional techniques.

Now, it's time to take our journey to the next level with A.C.E. – Accelerate, Crush, and Elevate – as our guiding principles. In the upcoming section, "Utilizing ChatGPT To Enhance Instructional Strategies And Methods," we will delve deeper into how ChatGPT can be your invaluable tool to A.C.E. your teaching evaluations.

By incorporating AI-powered prompts, we can access instant insights, innovative approaches, and time-saving strategies that will help us Accelerate our growth, Crush our goals, and Elevate our teaching practices. Let ChatGPT be your ultimate companion as we unlock the secrets to professional growth and student success.

So, let's get ready to A.C.E. our evaluations with ChatGPT by our side. Together, we will Accelerate our teaching effectiveness, Crush our evaluation challenges, and Elevate our instructional strategies to new heights. Join us on this transformative journey and discover the power of ChatGPT to A.C.E. your way to success!.

Utilizing ChatGPT To Enhance Instructional Strategies And Methods

Incorporating technology into teaching practices can greatly enhance instructional strategies and methods, providing new opportunities for engagement and learning. ChatGPT, as a powerful language model, can serve as a valuable tool for educators, offering support, generating ideas, and providing insights to enhance teaching effectiveness. In this section, we will explore how teachers can leverage ChatGPT to augment their instructional approaches, foster student engagement, and promote effective learning outcomes. With ChatGPT as a collaborative partner, educators can unlock innovative possibilities and enrich their teaching repertoire.

A. Communicating Consciously:

Effective communication is essential for fostering understanding and engagement in the classroom. This section focuses on three subcomponents of conscious communication: using clear and precise language, adapting communication for diverse learners, and providing clear directions and instructions. By honing these skills, teachers can create a cohesive and inclusive learning environment. Here are prompts to support your growth in each area:

Using Clear and Precise Language: Clear and precise language is the foundation of effective communication. By expressing thoughts, instructions, and explanations in a concise and understandable manner, teachers facilitate student comprehension. Here are prompts to help you improve your communication clarity:

Example Prompt:

Teacher: "Chat GPT, how can I simplify complex concepts without losing their depth and accuracy when explaining them to my students?"

Example Prompt:

Teacher: "Chat GPT, what techniques can I use to ensure my language is clear and precise when giving directions for experiments to my middle school students?"

Example Prompt:

Teacher: "Chat GPT, what are some effective strategies or techniques to simplify complex historical events and concepts when teaching them to high school students with varying levels of prior knowledge?"

Adapting Communication for Diverse Learners: Catering to the diverse needs of students is crucial for inclusive instruction. Adapting communication approaches ensures that all learners can access and engage with the content. Here are prompts to assist you in adapting your communication:

Example Prompt:

Teacher: "Chat GPT, what strategies can I implement to effectively communicate with visual learners who require visual aids?"

Example Prompt:

Teacher: "Chat GPT, how can I modify my communication approach to ensure that English language learners in my math class understand the concepts?"

Example Prompt:

Teacher: "Chat GPT, how can I modify my communication approach to effectively engage and support students with ADHD during whole-class discussions?"

Providing Clear Directions and Instructions: Clear directions and instructions empower students to navigate tasks and assignments successfully. By delivering concise and unambiguous guidance, teachers set students up for success. Here are prompts to help you refine your directions:

Example Prompt:

Teacher: "Chat GPT, what are practical ways to deliver clear instructions that help elementary students complete a group project effectively?"

Example Prompt:

Teacher: "Chat GPT, how can I ensure my instructions for solving math problems are easily comprehensible to students with different levels of prior knowledge?"

Example Prompt:

Teacher: "Chat GPT, what are some practical tips for delivering clear and concise instructions for hands-on science experiments that involve multiple steps and materials?"

By addressing these subcomponents and utilizing the provided prompts, teachers can enhance their communication skills, create an inclusive learning environment, and support student understanding and engagement.

B. Crafting Questions and Classroom Discourse:

Effective questioning techniques and fostering meaningful classroom discourse are essential for promoting critical thinking and engaging students in deep learning. Here are some strategies to help you master this component:

Asking Thought-Provoking Questions: Asking thought-provoking questions challenges students to think critically, analyze information, and articulate their ideas. Here are some prompts to enhance your ability to craft thought-provoking questions:

Example Prompt:

Teacher: "Chat GPT, what are some effective ways to structure questions that promote higher-order thinking skills in a social studies lesson about government systems?"

Example Prompt:

Teacher: Chat GPT, can you provide examples of open-ended questions that encourage students to explore multiple perspectives in a literature discussion?"

Example Prompt:

Teacher: "Chat GPT, how can I incorporate probing questions to deepen students' understanding of scientific concepts during a lab activity?"

Facilitating Student-Led Discussions: Student-led discussions empower students to take ownership of their learning, develop communication skills, and engage in collaborative problem-solving. Here are some prompts to guide you in facilitating effective student-led discussions:

Example Prompt:

Teacher: "Chat GPT, what strategies can I use to create a supportive environment where students feel comfortable sharing their opinions and respectfully challenging their peers during a class debate?"

Example Prompt:

Teacher: "Chat GPT, how can I encourage active participation and equal contribution from all students during a group discussion in a math class?"

Example Prompt:

Teacher: "Chat GPT, what are some effective ways to scaffold and facilitate small-group discussions to ensure that students stay focused and on-topic?"

Encouraging Active Participation:　Promoting active participation ensures that all students have opportunities to contribute to classroom discussions and share their perspectives. Here are some prompts to help you foster active participation among your students:

Example Prompt:

Teacher: "Chat GPT, what strategies can I use to engage introverted students and encourage their active participation in whole-class discussions?"

Example Prompt:

Teacher: "Chat GPT, how can I create an inclusive classroom environment that values diverse opinions and encourages students to express themselves during class discussions?"

Example Prompt:

Teacher: "Chat GPT, what are some techniques I can employ to motivate reluctant speakers and encourage them to actively participate in group activities or discussions?"

By incorporating these strategies and utilizing the provided prompts, you can enhance your questioning techniques, facilitate meaningful classroom discourse, and create an environment that fosters critical thinking and active engagement among your students.

C. Are Students Engaged?

Actively engaging students in the learning process is vital for fostering motivation, curiosity, and a deep understanding of the content. Here are some strategies to ensure that your students remain engaged:

Utilizing Instructional Strategies: Effective instructional strategies captivate students' attention and promote active participation. Here are some prompts to help you incorporate engaging instructional strategies:

Example Prompt:

Teacher: "Chat GPT, what are some innovative ways to introduce a new topic in a science lesson that will grab students' attention and spark their curiosity?"

Example Prompt:

Teacher: "Chat GPT, how can I structure a group activity in a history class to actively involve all students and make the learning experience more interactive?"

Example Prompt:

Teacher: "Chat GPT, what are some engaging strategies I can use to teach complex mathematical concepts and keep students motivated and focused?"

Incorporating Technology: Integrating technology into your lessons can enhance student engagement and provide interactive learning experiences. Here are some prompts to help you effectively incorporate technology:

Example Prompt:

Teacher: "Chat GPT, what are some educational apps or online tools that can facilitate active learning and student engagement in a language arts class?"

Example Prompt:

Teacher: "Chat GPT, how can I leverage multimedia resources such as videos, interactive simulations, or virtual field trips to enhance student engagement in a geography lesson?"

Example Prompt:

Teacher: "Chat GPT, what strategies can I use to promote digital collaboration and peer interaction in an online learning environment?"

Providing Hands-On Learning and Collaboration: Hands-on activities and collaborative learning experiences allow students to actively participate, explore, and apply their knowledge. Here are some prompts to guide you in providing hands-on learning and fostering collaboration:

Example Prompt:

Teacher: "Chat GPT, what are some hands-on experiments or activities I can incorporate into a science lesson to engage students in authentic learning and investigation?"

Example Prompt:

Teacher: "Chat GPT, how can I structure a project-based learning experience that promotes collaboration, problem-solving, and active engagement among students in a social studies class?"

Example Prompt:

Teacher: "Chat GPT, what are some strategies to facilitate productive group work and cooperative learning in a physical education setting?"

By implementing these strategies and utilizing the provided prompts, you can actively engage your students, promote their motivation and curiosity, and create a dynamic learning environment that fosters deep understanding and active participation.

D. Feedback for Improved Student Performance:

Providing constructive feedback is an essential aspect of promoting student growth and improvement. Effective feedback helps students understand their strengths and areas for improvement, guides their learning process, and enhances their overall performance. Here are some strategies to provide feedback that supports student growth:

Offering Specific and Actionable Feedback: Specific and actionable feedback provides students with clear guidance on how to enhance their performance. Here are some prompts to help you provide targeted feedback:

Example Prompt:

Teacher: "Chat GPT, how can I provide specific feedback to a student struggling with their writing skills to help them improve their organization and coherence?"

Example Prompt:

Teacher: "Chat GPT, what are some effective ways to offer actionable feedback to students in a math class to help them identify and correct errors in their problem-solving strategies?"

Example Prompt:

Teacher: "Chat GPT, how can I provide specific feedback to students during a group project to help them understand their individual contributions and areas for growth?"

Promoting Self-Assessment: Encouraging students to self-assess their work promotes metacognitive skills and empowers them to take ownership of their learning. Here are some prompts to guide self-assessment practices:

Example Prompt:

Teacher: "Chat GPT, how can I facilitate self-assessment in a science class to help students evaluate their own experimental procedures and draw conclusions from their findings?"

Example Prompt:

Teacher: "Chat GPT, what are some strategies to encourage students in a foreign language class to reflect on their speaking skills and identify areas they need to work on?"

Example Prompt:

Teacher: "Chat GPT, how can I support students in reflecting on their learning progress and setting goals for improvement in a physical education setting?"

Using Various Feedback Formats: Utilizing different feedback formats allows for a personalized approach and accommodates diverse student needs. Here are some prompts to help you explore various feedback formats:

Example Prompt:

Teacher: "Chat GPT, what are some effective ways to provide written feedback to students on their lab reports in a science class?"

Example Prompt:

Teacher: "Chat GPT, how can I incorporate peer feedback and peer assessment activities in a social studies class to promote collaboration and self-reflection?"

Example Prompt:

Teacher: "Chat GPT, what are some strategies to provide oral feedback during class discussions to guide students in developing their critical thinking and communication skills?"

By employing these feedback strategies and utilizing the provided prompts, you can support your students' growth, enhance their learning outcomes, and foster a culture of continuous improvement in your classroom.

E. Instructional Pivots and Responding to Emerging Student Needs:

Being responsive to emerging student needs and making instructional pivots is crucial for creating an inclusive and effective learning environment. It requires flexibility, awareness of individual student needs, and the ability to modify instructional strategies as necessary. Here are some approaches to help you respond to emerging student needs:

Adjusting Instructional Strategies Based on Student Feedback: Actively seeking and incorporating student feedback allows you to tailor your instruction to better meet their needs. Here are some prompts to guide you in adjusting your instructional strategies:

Example Prompt:

Teacher: "Chat GPT, how can I gather feedback from students to understand their learning preferences and adapt my teaching methods accordingly in a history class?"

Example Prompt:

Teacher: "Chat GPT, what are some strategies I can use to involve students in the process of shaping the curriculum and adjusting instructional methods in a project-based science class?"

Example Prompt:

Teacher: "Chat GPT, how can I modify my instructional strategies based on formative assessments to address the learning gaps of individual students in a language arts class?"

Differentiating Instruction: Differentiating instruction allows you to meet the diverse learning needs of your students by providing varied learning experiences and materials. Here are some prompts to help you differentiate your instruction:

Example Prompt:

Teacher: "Chat GPT, what are some effective ways to differentiate instruction for advanced learners in a mathematics class to challenge and extend their learning?"

Example Prompt:

Teacher: "Chat GPT, how can I provide additional support and scaffolding to students with special educational needs in a social studies class to help them access the curriculum?"

Example Prompt:

Teacher: "Chat GPT, what strategies can I use to offer choices and options in a literature class to accommodate diverse student interests and learning styles?"

Making Timely Modifications to Lesson Plans: Being open to making timely modifications to your lesson plans ensures that you address emerging student needs as they arise. Here are some prompts to guide you in making necessary modifications:

Example Prompt:

Teacher: "Chat GPT, how can I adapt my lesson plan in a physical education class to accommodate a student with a physical disability and ensure their active participation?"

Example Prompt:

Teacher: "Chat GPT, what are some strategies I can employ to modify a science experiment to make it more accessible for students with limited resources at home?"

Example Prompt:

Teacher: "Chat GPT, how can I make on-the-spot adjustments to my teaching strategies during a group project in a technology class to address conflicts and maximize collaboration?"

By employing these strategies and utilizing the provided prompts, you can effectively respond to emerging student needs, create an inclusive learning environment, and ensure that all students have equitable opportunities to thrive.

Incorporating ChatGPT into instructional strategies and methods can empower educators to create dynamic learning environments that cater to the diverse needs of students. By leveraging the power of ChatGPT, teachers can enhance their communication, promote student engagement, and adapt instruction to meet emerging student needs. As we have explored the A.C.E. concept throughout this section, we have seen how ChatGPT can assist in creating an Atmosphere of respect and rapport, crafting effective Classroom discourse, ensuring students are Engaged, providing Feedback for improved performance, and making Instructional pivots based on student needs. In the next section, "Generating Effective Dialogue With ChatGPT To Refine Instructional Practices," we will delve further into the dialogue with ChatGPT and explore how it can be harnessed to refine instructional practices and promote continuous improvement in teaching.

Generating Effective Dialogue With ChatGPT To Refine Instructional Practices

Engaging in reflective conversations with ChatGPT offers teachers a unique opportunity to analyze their teaching methods and approaches in a dynamic and interactive way. By leveraging ChatGPT's capabilities, educators can accelerate their professional growth, crush barriers to innovation, and elevate their instructional approaches. Through dialogue and collaboration, teachers can tap into ChatGPT's insights, seek feedback on lesson plans and materials, explore alternative strategies, and analyze student performance data to continuously improve their teaching practices. A.C.E. your evaluation by embracing these conversations with ChatGPT to drive instructional excellence and student success.

I. Leveraging ChatGPT for Reflective Dialogue

In this section, teachers engage in reflective dialogues with ChatGPT to deepen their understanding of instructional practices and refine their teaching approaches. Through these conversations, teachers critically analyze their own teaching methods, seek feedback and suggestions from ChatGPT, and explore innovative strategies to further enhance student learning. By leveraging ChatGPT as a reflective partner, teachers can continuously improve their teaching effectiveness and create impactful learning experiences for their students.

Engaging in reflective conversations with ChatGPT to analyze teaching methods and approaches provides teachers with a unique opportunity to analyze their teaching methods and approaches in a dynamic and interactive way. By engaging in dialogue with ChatGPT, teachers can explore their instructional practices, gain insights into their teaching effectiveness, and uncover new perspectives on pedagogy. This interactive process of reflection and dialogue with ChatGPT allows teachers to deepen their understanding of their own teaching and discover innovative ways to refine their instructional strategies for improved student outcomes.

Example Prompts/Dialogue:

Teacher: "ChatGPT, how can I improve my questioning techniques to elicit deeper student thinking during class discussions?"

Potential Response from ChatGPT: "One effective strategy is to use open-ended questions that require students to analyze, evaluate, or synthesize information. Additionally, incorporating wait time after asking a question allows students to process their thoughts before responding."

Example Feedback from Teacher: "Great suggestion! It's important to provide wait time for students to think before responding. Could you provide an example of an open-ended question that would promote deeper thinking during a discussion on literature analysis?"

Potential Response from ChatGPT: "Certainly! An example of an open-ended question could be: 'How does the author's use of symbolism contribute to the theme of the story? Provide specific evidence from the text to support your analysis."

Seeking feedback from ChatGPT on lesson plans and instructional materials opens up a valuable avenue for teachers to enhance their teaching practices. By actively engaging in conversations with ChatGPT, teachers can gain valuable insights and perspectives on their lesson plans, instructional materials, and overall instructional design. These reflective conversations provide teachers with an opportunity to refine their teaching strategies, identify areas for improvement, and explore innovative approaches to engage and support their students. The following prompts illustrate how teachers can leverage ChatGPT's feedback to strengthen their lesson plans and instructional materials, ultimately elevating the quality and impact of their teaching.

Example Prompts/Dialogue:

Teacher: "ChatGPT, can you review my lesson plan on fractions and suggest any improvements or additional activities?"

Potential Response from ChatGPT: "Your lesson plan looks comprehensive. To enhance student engagement, consider incorporating real-world examples of fractions and providing opportunities for hands-on activities. Additionally, you can include visual aids to support understanding."

Example Feedback from Teacher: "Thank you for your feedback! I appreciate the suggestion to include real-world examples. Could you provide an example of a hands-on activity that would help reinforce the concept of fractions?"

Potential Response from ChatGPT: "Certainly! An engaging hands-on activity could be to have students measure ingredients and follow a recipe to create a dish, where they have to convert measurements using fractions. This activity allows them to apply their understanding of fractions in a practical context."

II. Analyzing and Refining Instructional Approaches

Analyzing and refining instructional approaches through collaborative dialogue with ChatGPT empowers teachers to enhance their teaching practices and meet the diverse needs of their students. By engaging in reflective conversations with ChatGPT, teachers can explore and evaluate their current instructional approaches, seek feedback and suggestions, and uncover new strategies to optimize student engagement and learning outcomes. This section provides prompts that encourage teachers to collaborate with ChatGPT in developing differentiated instructional plans and explore alternative strategies, fostering continuous growth and improvement in their teaching practice.

Utilizing ChatGPT to explore alternative instructional strategies opens up a world of possibilities for teachers to innovate and adapt their teaching methods. By leveraging ChatGPT's insights and suggestions, teachers can expand their repertoire of instructional approaches, experiment with new techniques, and discover creative ways to engage and inspire their students. This section offers prompts that encourage teachers to tap into the potential of ChatGPT as a collaborative partner in exploring and refining their instructional strategies, ultimately enriching the teaching and learning experience.

Example Prompts/Dialogue:

Teacher: "ChatGPT, what are some creative approaches I can use to teach persuasive writing to high school students?"

Potential Response from ChatGPT: "One effective approach is to encourage students to analyze persuasive techniques used in real-world contexts, such as advertisements or speeches. You can also provide opportunities for students to engage in debates or write persuasive letters to a local authority."

Example Feedback from Teacher: "Thank you for the suggestions! Could you provide some specific examples of persuasive techniques commonly used in advertisements?"

Potential Response from ChatGPT: "Certainly! Some common persuasive techniques used in advertisements include emotional appeals, celebrity endorsements, and the use of catchy slogans or jingles. You can ask students to identify these techniques in advertisements they encounter and analyze their effectiveness."

Collaborating with ChatGPT to develop differentiated instructional plans empowers teachers to create tailored learning experiences that meet the diverse needs of their students. By engaging in collaborative dialogue with ChatGPT, teachers can leverage its expertise to brainstorm ideas, explore innovative strategies, and design instructional plans that promote personalized learning. This section provides prompts that demonstrate how teachers can collaborate with ChatGPT to develop differentiated instructional plans, accelerating their ability to meet the unique needs of every learner in their classroom.

Example Prompts/Dialogue:

Teacher: "ChatGPT, how can I differentiate instruction to meet the needs of both advanced learners and struggling students in my class?"

Potential Response from ChatGPT: "One strategy is to provide enrichment activities for advanced learners, such as extension projects or research opportunities. For students who need more assistance, consider offering additional support through small-group instruction or guided practice."

Example Feedback from Teacher: "I appreciate your suggestions. How can I ensure that the small-group instruction is effective in supporting struggling students' learning needs?"

Potential Response from ChatGPT: "To ensure the effectiveness of small-group instruction, you can carefully select appropriate instructional materials and tasks that target specific areas of difficulty for struggling students. Additionally, providing clear learning objectives and monitoring student progress through formative assessments can help tailor the instruction to their needs."

By taking the example dialogues one step further, teachers can receive additional guidance and support from ChatGPT to refine their instructional practices.

III. Analyzing Student Data and ChatGPT's Insights

In this section, teachers engage in meaningful conversations with ChatGPT to analyze student data and gain valuable insights. Through these dialogues, teachers address specific challenges and seek guidance on improving student performance. By leveraging ChatGPT's expertise, teachers can make data-informed decisions and enhance their instructional strategies for greater student success.

Discussing student performance data with ChatGPT and seeking insights for improvement offers teachers a valuable opportunity to analyze student progress and make data-informed instructional decisions. By engaging in dialogue with ChatGPT, teachers can share student data, discuss trends and patterns, and seek insights to refine their instructional practices. This section provides prompts that demonstrate how teachers can effectively discuss student performance data with ChatGPT, facilitating a collaborative process of analysis and reflection to elevate their teaching strategies and enhance student outcomes.

Example Prompts/Dialogue:

Teacher: "ChatGPT, based on the recent assessment data, how can I address the common misconceptions among my students regarding fractions?"

Potential Response from ChatGPT: "One approach is to provide targeted reteaching of specific concepts that students struggled with. You can also incorporate hands-on manipulatives or visual representations to enhance their understanding."

Example Feedback from Teacher: "Thank you for your insights. How can I effectively integrate hands-on manipulatives into my fraction lessons?"

Potential Response from ChatGPT: "To effectively integrate manipulatives, you can provide students with physical objects like fraction blocks or pie charts that they can manipulate and explore. Additionally, you can design activities where students have to represent and compare fractions using these manipulatives."

Continuing the dialogue with ChatGPT helps teachers gain further guidance and actionable strategies to refine their instructional practices. Through this interactive process, teachers can enhance their teaching methods, address specific challenges, and create more effective learning experiences for their students.

Incorporating ChatGPT's feedback and engaging in reflective dialogue provides educators with powerful tools to continuously refine their instructional practices. By embracing the A.C.E. approach of Accelerating their growth, Crushing barriers to innovation, and Elevating their teaching strategies, teachers can harness the potential of ChatGPT to enhance their effectiveness in the classroom. Through collaborative conversations, seeking feedback, exploring alternative approaches, and analyzing student performance data, educators can foster a culture of continuous improvement. By leveraging the insights and support of ChatGPT, teachers can take their instructional practices to new heights, ultimately leading to better student outcomes and a more impactful learning experience. So let's A.C.E. our evaluation and embrA.C.E. the power of ChatGPT to elevate our teaching and shape the future of education.

Incorporating ChatGPT Feedback For Continuous Improvement In Instruction

In the journey towards continuous improvement in instruction, ChatGPT can serve as a valuable tool to provide insights, suggestions, and feedback that guide teachers in refining their instructional practices. By leveraging ChatGPT's AI capabilities, educators can enhance their ability to A.C.E. the evaluation process and accelerate their professional growth. This section explores how teachers can incorporate ChatGPT feedback into each stage of the continuous improvement cycle, from data analysis to action planning and implementation.

I. Data Analysis:
Analyzing data is a crucial step in the continuous improvement cycle. By seeking ChatGPT's assistance, teachers can gain valuable insights and alternative perspectives on the data they have collected. Here are some prompts to guide data analysis with ChatGPT:

Example Prompts/Dialogue:

Teacher: "ChatGPT, based on the assessment results, how can I identify patterns and trends to determine areas where students are struggling and need additional support?"

ChatGPT: "You can analyze the assessment data by looking for common misconceptions, specific question types with lower performance, or patterns of incorrect responses. This will help you identify the specific areas where students may need further clarification and support."

II. Reflection and Goal Setting:
Reflecting on instructional practices and setting meaningful goals are essential for growth. ChatGPT can provide valuable prompts and feedback to support teachers in this process. Here are some prompts to facilitate reflection and goal setting with ChatGPT:

Example Prompts/Dialogue:

Teacher: "ChatGPT, after reflecting on my recent lesson, what specific areas should I focus on for improvement, and how can I set SMART goals to address them?"

ChatGPT: "Based on your reflection, you could focus on increasing student engagement during independent practice. A SMART goal could be to implement strategies such as incorporating interactive activities, providing clear instructions, and offering immediate feedback to enhance student involvement and understanding."

III. Action Planning and Implementation:

Developing action plans and effectively implementing changes are crucial for continuous improvement. ChatGPT can provide innovative strategies and suggestions to support teachers in their action planning process. Here are some prompts for action planning and implementation with ChatGPT:

Example Prompts/Dialogue:

Teacher: "ChatGPT, what are some effective instructional strategies I can employ to differentiate instruction and meet the diverse learning needs of my students?"

ChatGPT: "You can consider incorporating flexible grouping, offering varied learning materials, and providing multiple entry points to accommodate different learning styles and abilities. These strategies can help you create a more inclusive and engaging learning environment."

IV. Monitoring and Evaluation:

Monitoring the effectiveness of instructional changes and evaluating their impact is essential for continuous improvement. ChatGPT can offer insights and feedback on monitoring and evaluation strategies. Here are some prompts for monitoring and evaluation with ChatGPT:

Example Prompts/Dialogue:

Teacher: "ChatGPT, what are effective ways to collect formative feedback from students during instruction to gauge their understanding and progress?"

ChatGPT: "You can employ strategies such as exit tickets, quick quizzes, or digital tools that allow students to provide immediate feedback on their understanding. This will enable you to make timely adjustments to your instruction and better meet the needs of your students."

By incorporating ChatGPT into each stage of the continuous improvement cycle, teachers can benefit from its AI-powered insights, suggestions, and feedback to refine their instructional practices, maximize student learning outcomes, and continuously elevate their teaching effectiveness.

V. Reflection and Feedback:

Engaging in reflective conversations and seeking feedback from ChatGPT can provide valuable insights and alternative perspectives for teachers during the continuous improvement process. Here are prompts to guide reflection and feedback with ChatGPT:

Example Prompts/Dialogue:

Teacher: "ChatGPT, after implementing the new instructional strategy, what evidence should I look for to determine its effectiveness, and how can I reflect on the impact on student learning?"

ChatGPT: ChatGPT: "When evaluating the effectiveness of the new instructional strategy, look for changes in student engagement, performance on assessments, and their ability to apply the concepts learned. Reflection can involve analyzing the data, seeking student input, and reflecting on your observations to assess the impact on student learning."

VI. Iteration and Adjustment:

Continuously iterating and making adjustments based on data and feedback is crucial for instructional improvement. ChatGPT can offer suggestions and insights to support teachers in the iteration process. Here are prompts for iteration and adjustment with ChatGPT:

Example Prompts/Dialogue:

Teacher: "ChatGPT, I have implemented the suggested adjustments based on the feedback received. How can I monitor and assess the impact of these changes on student learning?"

ChatGPT: "To monitor the impact of the adjustments, you can use formative assessments, observations, and student feedback to gather data on their progress. Analyze the data to determine if the changes have positively influenced student learning outcomes and make further adjustments as needed."

By incorporating ChatGPT into the reflection, feedback, iteration, and adjustment stages of the continuous improvement cycle, teachers can leverage AI-powered insights and feedback to enhance their instructional practices, address student needs, and achieve continuous growth and improvement in their teaching effectiveness.

Impressive Instruction has taken you on a journey to explore the power of Chat GPT in enhancing instructional strategies and methods. Through the A.C.E. concept, you have discovered how Chat GPT can accelerate your teaching success, help you crush your teaching goals, and elevate your teaching practices to new heights. By leveraging AI prompts, insights, and feedback, you have learned how to continuously improve your instruction, meet the diverse needs of your students, and maximize student outcomes. As we conclude this episode, you are now equipped with the knowledge and tools to A.C.E. your evaluations and elevate your teaching effectiveness. In the next episode, we will shift our focus to the importance of professionalism in the teaching profession and explore how Chat GPT can support your growth as a professional educator.

Episode Four
Teacher Professionalism: The Digital Mastery

Understanding The Components of Teacher Professionalism

Professionalism plays a critical role in a teacher's overall effectiveness and impact. In this episode, we will explore the essential components of teacher professionalism and how Chat GPT can assist educators in cultivating and strengthening their professional practice. As you embark on this journey of professional growth - remember to A.C.E. your evaluation - by taking the time to pause and reflect on your craft, maintaining record keeping with integrity, establishing successful communication with families, adding additional value to your district and school community, prioritizing professional growth, and demonstrating your professionalism in all aspects of your work.

A. Take Time to Pause and Reflect on Your Craft:
Reflective practice is key to professional growth and improvement. Chat GPT can provide prompts and guidance to help you engage in meaningful self-reflection, analyze your teaching practices, and identify areas for enhancement. By taking time to pause and reflect, you can refine your instructional approaches, increase your effectiveness, and ultimately improve student outcomes.

B. Record Keeping with Integrity:
Accurate and organized record keeping is essential for maintaining professionalism. Chat GPT can offer innovative strategies for managing and organizing your records, ensuring their integrity and accessibility. By leveraging AI-powered prompts, you can streamline your record-keeping processes, track student progress effectively, and maintain a comprehensive overview of your teaching practice.

C. Successful Communication with Families:
Building strong partnerships with families is crucial for student success. Chat GPT can provide prompts and suggestions to enhance your communication skills, whether through written correspondence, parent-teacher conferences, or digital platforms. By fostering effective communication with families, you can create a supportive learning environment and promote collaborative relationships.

D. Adding Additional Value to Your District and School Community:

Being a professional educator involves actively contributing to your school community and district. Chat GPT can offer insights and ideas to help you add value, whether through participating in school events, leading professional development sessions, or engaging in community outreach. By going above and beyond your classroom responsibilities, you can make a positive impact on your school community and contribute to its overall success.

E. Professional Growth:

Continual professional growth is essential for staying current and improving as an educator. Chat GPT can provide personalized recommendations, resources, and insights to support your professional development journey. By embracing opportunities for growth, such as attending workshops, pursuing advanced certifications, or engaging in online learning, you can enhance your skills, expand your knowledge, and continually elevate your teaching practice.

F. Demonstrating You are a Professional:

Exemplifying professionalism in all aspects of your work is vital. Chat GPT can provide guidance on demonstrating professionalism through your actions, interactions with colleagues and students, and adherence to ethical standards. By upholding high standards of professionalism, you inspire trust and confidence in your abilities as an educator.

As you incorporate Chat GPT into your professional journey, remember to leverage its AI-powered prompts and guidance to accelerate your growth, crush your goals, and elevate your professionalism. By embracing these components of teacher professionalism, you can foster a positive learning environment, strengthen your relationships with students and families, and make a lasting impact on the educational community. Now, let's explore each component in detail and discover how Chat GPT can support you in embodying the highest standards of teacher professionalism.c

Unpacking The Indicators And Professional Obligations

.A. Take Time to Pause and Reflect on Your Craft
Reflective practice is a vital component of professional growth for teachers. By taking time to pause and reflect on their craft, educators can gain valuable insights, identify

areas for improvement, and enhance student learning outcomes. Whether you are a seasoned teacher or new to the profession, engaging in reflective practices can benefit your teaching approach. Here are two example prompt/dialogues to support your reflective journey:

Example Prompts/Dialogue:

Teacher: "ChatGPT, how can I deepen the accuracy and depth of my reflections on lessons, providing specific examples?"

ChatGPT: "To deepen the accuracy and depth of your reflections on lessons and provide specific examples, consider the following approaches:

- Regularly review student work samples and assess their progress. Identify patterns, strengths, and areas for improvement. Refer to specific examples of student work to support your reflections.
- Keep a reflective journal or use a digital platform to document your thoughts, observations, and specific instances that stood out during lessons. These examples will help you analyze and evaluate your teaching methods.
- Engage in collaborative discussions with colleagues. Share specific examples of successful teaching strategies and challenges you encountered. Seek their perspectives and insights to deepen your reflections.
- Seek feedback from your students through surveys, questionnaires, or classroom discussions. Ask them to provide specific examples of what worked well or what they found challenging. Use their responses to inform your reflections.
- Continuously expand your pedagogical repertoire by exploring professional development opportunities. Use your knowledge and experience to suggest alternative strategies in your reflections."

Example Prompts/Dialogue:

Teacher: "ChatGPT, how can I draw upon my bank of knowledge/experiences to suggest alternative strategies in my reflections?"

ChatGPT: "To draw upon your bank of knowledge/experiences and suggest alternative strategies in your reflections, consider the following suggestions:

- Reflect on your past experiences across different content areas and grade levels. Identify instances where you successfully addressed challenges or engaged students effectively. Use these experiences as a foundation for suggesting alternative strategies.
- Stay updated on current research, educational trends, and innovative instructional approaches. Explore literature and attend professional development sessions to gather insights into effective teaching strategies. Incorporate these insights into your reflections and propose alternative strategies aligned with best practices.
- Collaborate with colleagues from various content areas and grade levels. Engage in discussions that explore alternative strategies used in different contexts. Share and learn from each other's experiences to expand your repertoire.
- Seek feedback from students, parents, or other stakeholders. Gain different perspectives on your teaching methods and ask for specific examples of what resonated with them or what they found challenging. Use their insights to suggest alternative strategies that cater to diverse needs.
- Embrace technology tools and resources that can enhance your instructional practices. Explore digital platforms, educational apps, or online resources that align with your content area and grade level. Reflect on their impact and suggest alternative strategies based on their effectiveness."

Remember, these prompts are designed to support teachers at various experience levels and across different content areas and grade levels. EmbrA.C.E. the opportunity to reflect on your teaching practice and leverage your diverse background knowledge as you engage with these prompts.

B. Record Keeping with Integrity

Accurate record keeping is essential for effective classroom management and student assessment. Teachers must maintain an efficient and effective system for record keeping while ensuring the privacy and security of student information in compliance with federal, state, local, and district policies. Additionally, involving students in the maintenance of records as appropriate can promote their ownership of learning and foster a sense of responsibility. Here are two example prompt/dialogues to support your record keeping practices:

Example Prompts/Dialogue:

Teacher: "ChatGPT, how can I maintain accurate records efficiently and effectively while adhering to privacy and data rules?"

ChatGPT: "To maintain accurate records efficiently and effectively while adhering to privacy and data rules, consider the following strategies:

- Establish a systematic and organized approach to record keeping. Create digital or physical folders for each student and subject area, ensuring easy access and retrieval of information.
- Use a digital gradebook or record-keeping platform that complies with privacy regulations and offers secure data storage. Familiarize yourself with the features and functionalities of the platform to optimize your record keeping process.
- Regularly update and review your records to ensure accuracy. Allocate specific time slots in your schedule for record maintenance, such as after each assessment or grading period.
- Communicate with students and parents about the importance of record keeping and their roles in its maintenance. Clearly explain privacy protocols and expectations for handling sensitive information.
- Implement anonymized systems for data entry when using digital tools or platforms. Avoid entering student identifying information in ChatGPT or any other AI-powered systems to safeguard student privacy.
- Stay informed about federal, state, local, and district policies related to data privacy and security. Attend professional development sessions or consult resources provided by your educational institution to remain up to date with the latest guidelines."

Example Prompts/Dialogue:

Teacher: "ChatGPT, how can I involve students in maintaining accurate records and promote their ownership of learning?"

ChatGPT: "To involve students in maintaining accurate records and promote their ownership of learning, consider the following approaches:

- Explain to students the purpose and importance of record keeping in their educational journey. Help them understand how records reflect their progress and serve as evidence of their growth.
- Assign specific responsibilities to students related to record keeping, such as entering completed assignments or tracking their own progress. Provide clear instructions and guidelines to ensure accuracy and consistency.
- Teach students how to set goals and monitor their own learning. Encourage them to reflect on their achievements and challenges, and record their observations in their personal portfolios or learning journals.
- Foster a collaborative classroom culture where students support each other in maintaining records. Implement peer-review processes where students provide constructive feedback on their peers' work and progress.
- Incorporate reflection and self-assessment activities into the record-keeping process. Encourage students to analyze their performance, identify areas for improvement, and set goals for future learning.
- Emphasize the importance of privacy and confidentiality. Teach students to respect the privacy of their peers' information and model appropriate behavior in handling sensitive data.

Remember, when using ChatGPT or any other AI-powered system, never enter student identifying information to ensure student privacy is protected. By following privacy and data rules and involving students in the record-keeping process, you can maintain accurate records while promoting a sense of ownership and responsibility among your students.

C. Successful Communication with Families

Effective communication with families is crucial for building strong partnerships and supporting students' educational journey. Teachers who communicate frequently and sensitively with families can successfully engage them in the instructional program, fostering collaboration and shared responsibility. Additionally, involving students in the communication process empowers them to actively participate in sharing their learning experiences with their families. Here are two example prompt/dialogues to enhance your communication practices with families:

Example Prompts/Dialogue:

Teacher: "ChatGPT, how can I communicate frequently and sensitively with families to engage them in the instructional program?"

ChatGPT: To communicate frequently and sensitively with families and engage them in the instructional program, consider the following strategies:

- Establish multiple channels of communication, such as email, phone calls, parent-teacher conferences, and digital platforms. Provide families with options to choose the mode of communication that suits their preferences and needs.
- Develop a communication plan to ensure regular updates on students' progress, upcoming events, and classroom activities. Share newsletters, weekly summaries, or class websites to keep families informed and involved.
- Be proactive in reaching out to families, especially when there are important updates or concerns regarding students' academic or social-emotional well-being. Timely communication shows that you value their partnership and are committed to their child's success.
- Demonstrate sensitivity and cultural responsiveness in your communication. Consider diverse family backgrounds and perspectives, and strive to create an inclusive environment where all families feel valued and respected.
- Encourage two-way communication by inviting families to share their insights, questions, or concerns. Actively listen and respond empathetically, addressing their needs and providing support when necessary.
- Collaborate with families in decision-making processes related to their child's education. Seek their input in setting goals, developing strategies, and evaluating progress to foster a sense of ownership and shared responsibility."

Example Prompts/Dialogue:

Teacher: "ChatGPT, how can I involve students in communicating with their families to share their learning experiences?"

ChatGPT: "To involve students in communicating with their families and sharing their learning experiences, consider the following approaches:

- Teach students about the importance of family communication and how it contributes to their educational journey. Help them understand that sharing their achievements, challenges, and goals with their families strengthens the support network.
- Provide opportunities for students to reflect on their learning and articulate their experiences. Encourage them to create portfolios, presentations, or written reflections that showcase their progress and share them with their families.
- Incorporate student-led conferences or presentations where students take the lead in communicating their learning to their families. Support them in preparing and articulating their thoughts effectively.
- Integrate digital platforms or learning management systems that allow students to showcase their work and communicate with their families. Encourage students to share their projects, assignments, or reflections digitally.
- Foster a classroom environment that values student voice and collaboration. Incorporate group projects or discussions where students work together to develop presentations or reports that can be shared with their families.
- Provide guidance and support to students in expressing their thoughts and feelings effectively. Help them use appropriate language, tone, and structure when communicating with their families.

Remember, when communicating with families, respect their privacy and adhere to any relevant privacy laws or policies. By communicating frequently, sensitively, and involving students in the process, you can successfully engage families in the instructional program and promote a collaborative partnership for student success.

D. Adding Additional Value to Your District and School Community

Teachers play a vital role not only within their classrooms but also in contributing to the overall success and growth of their school and district community. They actively engage in school and district events and projects, assuming leadership positions and collaborating with colleagues to make a substantial impact. Here is an example prompt/dialogue to inspire teachers to add value to their community:

Example Prompts/Dialogue:

Teacher: "ChatGPT, how can I make a substantial contribution to school and district events and projects while assuming leadership with my colleagues?"

ChatGPT: "To make a substantial contribution to school and district events and projects while assuming leadership with your colleagues, consider the following strategies:

- Actively participate in school and district committees, task forces, or professional learning communities. Offer your expertise and insights to help shape initiatives and projects that align with the goals of the school and district.
- Seek leadership opportunities within your school, such as serving as a department head, instructional coach, or mentor teacher. Take on responsibilities that allow you to support and guide your colleagues in their professional growth.
- Collaborate with colleagues on curriculum development, instructional strategies, or assessment practices. Share your ideas, resources, and best practices to enhance teaching and learning across the school or district.
- Volunteer to organize or contribute to school-wide events, such as parent-teacher conferences, open houses, or cultural celebrations. Offer your skills and creativity to make these events engaging and memorable for the entire school community.
- Share your expertise through professional development workshops or presentations. Offer to lead sessions on topics you are knowledgeable about, providing valuable learning experiences for your colleagues.
- Engage in community partnerships and outreach programs. Collaborate with local organizations or businesses to create opportunities for students and connect classroom learning with real-world experiences.
- Stay informed about district-wide initiatives, policies, and goals. Be an advocate for your school and district, actively participating in discussions and decision-making processes that shape the educational landscape.
- Foster a collaborative culture by sharing resources, ideas, and successes with your colleagues so that everyone feels valued and empowered to contribute."

Remember, as you assume leadership and contribute to school and district events and projects, ensure that you collaborate effectively with your colleagues and respect their perspectives. By actively engaging in these opportunities, you can make a substantial difference in your school and district community, fostering growth and success for all stakeholders involved.

E. Professional Growth

Teachers who are committed to their professional growth continuously seek opportunities to enhance their knowledge, skills, and practices. They actively contribute to the profession through activities like action research and mentoring new teachers, while actively pursuing professional development. Here are example prompts/dialogues to inspire teachers to engage in meaningful professional growth:

Example Prompts/Dialogue:

Teacher: "ChatGPT, how can I make a substantial contribution to the profession through action research?"

ChatGPT: "To make a substantial contribution to the profession through action research, consider the following steps:

- Identify an area of interest or a specific challenge within your teaching practice that you would like to investigate further.
- Conduct a thorough literature review to explore existing research and best practices related to your chosen area.
- Develop a research question or hypothesis that will guide your action research project.
- Collect relevant data through observations, surveys, interviews, or other appropriate methods.
- Analyze the data and draw meaningful conclusions that inform your teaching practice.
- Share your findings with colleagues, either through presentations, publications, or informal discussions.
- Reflect on the impact of your action research and consider potential next steps for further exploration or improvement.
- Remember, action research is a collaborative process, so consider seeking feedback and input from colleagues or engaging in a professional learning community to enrich your research experience."

Example Prompts/Dialogue:

Teacher: "ChatGPT, how can I effectively mentor new teachers?"

ChatGPT: "To effectively mentor new teachers, consider the following strategies:

- Establish a supportive and trusting relationship with the new teacher. Create a safe space for open communication and collaboration.
- Share your experiences, challenges, and successes as a teacher. Provide insights and practical tips to help the new teacher navigate their early years.
- Observe and provide constructive feedback on the new teacher's lessons. Offer specific suggestions for improvement while highlighting their strengths.
- Help the new teacher develop their instructional skills by sharing resources, model lessons, and effective teaching strategies.
- Collaborate on lesson planning and curriculum development, ensuring the new teacher feels supported and empowered in their role.
- Encourage reflection and self-assessment. Help the new teacher set goals and create an action plan for their professional growth.
- Foster connections between the new teacher and the broader professional community. Introduce them to relevant professional organizations, conferences, or online networks.
- Continuously support and encourage the new teacher, celebrating their achievements and helping them navigate any challenges they encounter.
- Remember, mentoring is a reciprocal process, so be open to learning from the new teacher as well. Your guidance and support can have a profound impact on their professional development."

Example Prompts/Dialogue:

Teacher: "ChatGPT, how can I actively pursue professional development?"

ChatGPT: "To actively pursue professional development, consider the following approaches:

- Set clear goals for your professional growth. Identify areas where you would like to expand your knowledge or skills.
- Seek out relevant workshops, conferences, or webinars that align with your goals. Participate actively, take notes, and reflect on how you can apply what you have learned in your classroom.
- Engage in online learning platforms or courses that offer flexible and self-paced professional development opportunities.
- Join professional organizations or associations in your subject area or grade level. Attend their events, participate in discussions, and take advantage of the resources they offer.
- Create a professional learning network by connecting with colleagues both within and outside of your school. Share resources, engage in collaborative projects, and learn from each other's experiences.
- Explore educational literature, research articles, and blogs to stay updated on current trends and best practices in education.

F. Demonstrating You are a Professional

Teachers who demonstrate professionalism take on leadership roles to ensure that school practices and procedures honor the needs of all students, especially those who have been traditionally underserved. They actively advocate for equity and inclusivity within their school community. Here are example prompts/dialogues to support teachers in demonstrating their professionalism:

Example Prompts/Dialogue:

Teacher: "ChatGPT, how can I assume a leadership position in ensuring that school practices and procedures honor all students, particularly those traditionally underserved?"

ChatGPT: "To assume a leadership position in honoring all students, particularly those traditionally underserved, consider the following strategies:

- Educate yourself about the needs and experiences of marginalized or underserved student populations. Familiarize yourself with research, resources, and best practices in culturally responsive teaching and inclusive education.
- Collaborate with colleagues, administrators, and other stakeholders to review and analyze school practices and procedures. Identify areas where improvements can be made to better meet the needs of all students.
- Advocate for changes in policies or practices that may perpetuate inequities or disparities. Present evidence-based arguments and propose alternative approaches that promote equity and inclusivity.
- Lead or participate in professional development sessions focused on culturally responsive teaching, social justice, or inclusive pedagogies. Share your knowledge and experiences with colleagues to inspire collective growth and change.
- Actively seek opportunities to engage in conversations about equity and inclusion within your school community. Encourage dialogue, empathy, and understanding among staff, students, and families.
- Collaborate with community organizations or stakeholders to develop partnerships that support the needs of underserved students and families. Foster connections that extend beyond the school walls.
- Serve as a mentor or guide for colleagues who are interested in learning more about culturally responsive practices. Offer support, resources, and guidance as they navigate their own professional journey towards inclusivity.
- Remember, leading with a commitment to equity and inclusivity requires ongoing reflection, learning, and collaboration with others. By assuming a leadership position, you can contribute to a more equitable and empowering school environment."

Example Prompts/Dialogue:

Teacher: "ChatGPT, how can I advocate for the needs of traditionally underserved students within my school?"

ChatGPT: "To advocate for the needs of traditionally underserved students, consider the following steps:

- Develop a deep understanding of the unique challenges and strengths of the student populations you aim to support. Listen to their voices, experiences, and perspectives to inform your advocacy efforts.
- Identify specific areas where support and resources may be lacking for underserved students. This could include access to advanced coursework, culturally relevant curriculum materials, or targeted interventions.
- Collaborate with colleagues, administrators, and families to raise awareness about these needs and initiate conversations about potential solutions. Use data and research to support your arguments and proposals.
- Engage in professional learning opportunities focused on equity, culturally responsive practices, and strategies for supporting underserved students. Share your learnings with colleagues and encourage them to join you in this journey.
- Actively participate in school committees or task forces that address issues of equity and inclusivity. Provide input, contribute ideas, and advocate for policy changes or initiatives that prioritize the needs of underserved students.
- Foster positive relationships with families and community organizations that represent traditionally underserved populations. Collaborate to develop strategies that promote their active involvement in the school community.
- Amplify the voices of underserved students and their families by creating opportunities for them to share their experiences and perspectives. Use platforms like student-led conferences, parent-teacher associations, or cultural celebrations to ensure their voices are heard.

Remember, advocacy is a continuous process that requires empathy, perseverance, and a commitment to dismantling systemic barriers that hinder the success of underserved students.

In this section, we have delved into the indicators and professional obligations that contribute to teachers' growth and success. Through applying ChatGPT prompts teachers can A.C.E. their evaluations and - Accelerate their professional growth, Crush their teaching goals, and Elevate their instructional practices. By leveraging ChatGPT as a trusted companion, teachers can access instant insights, time-saving strategies, and innovative approaches to enhance their teaching effectiveness.

With ChatGPT as a powerful AI tool, teachers can unlock a wealth of knowledge and resources to propel their professional growth and improve student outcomes. By aligning teaching practices with the evaluation framework and utilizing AI-powered prompts, teachers can A.C.E. their evaluations, overcome challenges, and excel in the classroom. By incorporating ChatGPT into their teaching approach, teachers can elevate their instructional strategies, engage students effectively, and create exceptional learning environments. With cutting-edge resources, personalized recommendations, and AI-driven insights, teachers can take their teaching to the next level and deliver exceptional results.

As we move forward, we will explore how ChatGPT can maximize its potential in managing professional responsibilities. From organizing schedules and collaborating with colleagues to accessing resources and streamlining administrative tasks, ChatGPT can be a valuable tool in supporting teachers' diverse demands. Let's continue our journey and discover the transformative power of ChatGPT in managing professional responsibilities..

Maximizing ChatGPT's Potential In Managing Professional Responsibilities

As educators strive to manage their professional responsibilities effectively, maximizing the potential of ChatGPT can be a game-changer. By leveraging AI-powered prompts, teachers can streamline tasks, access resources, collaborate with colleagues, and enhance their overall efficiency. The benefits of integrating ChatGPT into their professional practice are numerous, offering time-saving strategies, innovative approaches, and instant insights to support their professional growth and development.

Streamlining Administrative Tasks: ChatGPT can be a valuable tool in managing various administrative tasks, including record-keeping, lesson planning, and documentation. By leveraging its capabilities, teachers can streamline these processes and save time. Here are some prompts to support you as a teacher in optimizing your use of ChatGPT for administrative efficiency:

Example Prompt:

Teacher: "Chat GPT, how can I effectively utilize AI prompts to streamline my record-keeping process?"

Example Prompt:

Teacher: "Chat GPT, what are some innovative ways ChatGPT can help me organize my lesson plans and resources?"

Example Prompt:

Teacher: "Chat GPT, how can I leverage ChatGPT to streamline documentation and paperwork, such as grading and assessment records?"

By exploring these prompts and engaging in discussions with ChatGPT, you can uncover valuable insights and strategies to enhance your administrative tasks. Whether it's finding new approaches to organize your records, discovering innovative methods for lesson planning, or simplifying your documentation process, ChatGPT is here to support you every step of the way.

Enhancing Collaboration and Communication: Collaboration and communication are essential components of our professional responsibilities as teachers. ChatGPT can play a valuable role in facilitating effective collaboration and communication among colleagues, administrators, and support staff. Here are some prompts to support you in utilizing ChatGPT to enhance collaboration and communication:

Example Prompt:

Teacher: "ChatGPT, what are some effective ways to collaborate with colleagues using AI-powered tools?"

Example Prompt:

Teacher: "How can ChatGPT assist me in communicating with parents and engaging them in the instructional program?"

Example Prompt:

Teacher: "What are some innovative approaches for utilizing ChatGPT to enhance communication with administrators and support staff?"

By exploring these prompts and engaging in interactive discussions with ChatGPT, you can discover new ways to collaborate with your colleagues, strengthen relationships with parents, and improve communication with administrators and support staff.

Accessing and Sharing Resources: Accessing a wide range of resources is crucial for our professional growth and development as teachers. ChatGPT offers an incredible opportunity to tap into a vast pool of knowledge and access various resources, including research articles, lesson plans, and professional development materials. Here are some prompts to assist you in effectively utilizing ChatGPT for accessing and sharing resources:

Example Prompt:

Teacher: "ChatGPT, how can I leverage AI prompts to find relevant research articles and resources for my content area?"

Example Prompt:

Teacher: "What are some strategies for utilizing ChatGPT to discover and adapt high-quality lesson plans?"

Example Prompt:

Teacher: "How can I maximize ChatGPT's potential in accessing professional development materials and staying updated with current trends in education?"

By engaging in interactive discussions with ChatGPT and exploring these prompts, you can uncover valuable resources, stay informed about the latest research and teaching practices, and access high-quality lesson plans tailored to your content area. Embrace the power of ChatGPT as a tool for resource discovery, adaptation, and sharing, and enhance your teaching practices with a wealth of knowledge at your fingertips. Let's make the most of ChatGPT's potential to access and share resources that will empower us as educators and benefit our students' learning experiences.

Managing Time and Prioritizing Tasks: As an educator, managing our time effectively and prioritizing tasks are essential for maintaining a healthy work-life balance. ChatGPT can serve as a valuable tool in supporting us in these areas, offering insights and strategies to optimize our time management. Here are some prompts to help you utilize ChatGPT to optimize your time management:

Example Prompt:

Teacher: "ChatGPT, what are some time-saving strategies I can implement in my daily teaching responsibilities?"

Example Prompt:

Teacher:"How can ChatGPT assist me in prioritizing tasks and creating efficient schedules?"

Example Prompt:

Teacher:"What are some innovative approaches for utilizing ChatGPT to manage my professional responsibilities while maintaining a work-life balance?"

By engaging in interactive discussions with ChatGPT and exploring these prompts, you can discover practical strategies for maximizing your productivity, identify methods to prioritize tasks effectively, and explore innovative approaches to manage your professional responsibilities. ChatGPT can offer insights and suggestions tailored to your specific needs and challenges, helping you make the most of your time and achieve a healthy balance between your professional and personal life. Let's leverage the power of ChatGPT to enhance our time management skills and create a fulfilling teaching experience.

Reflective Practice and Professional Growth: Reflective practice is a crucial component of professional growth for educators, and ChatGPT can be a valuable partner in this journey. By leveraging AI prompts, ChatGPT can provide insights, feedback, and self-reflection prompts that support our continuous improvement and development as teachers. Here are some prompts to support you in leveraging ChatGPT for reflective practice and professional growth:

Example Prompt:

Teacher: "ChatGPT, how can I use AI prompts to enhance my self-reflection and improve my teaching practices?"

Example Prompt:

Teacher: "What are some effective ways ChatGPT can provide feedback and insights on my instructional approaches?"

Example Prompt:

Teacher: "How can I incorporate ChatGPT into my professional growth plan and actively pursue continuous improvement?"

Engaging in interactive discussions with ChatGPT using these prompts can help you gain valuable insights, challenge your assumptions, and encourage deep reflection on your teaching practices. By incorporating ChatGPT into your reflective practice, you can receive personalized feedback and suggestions tailored to your teaching context, explore innovative ideas, and identify areas for growth. Let ChatGPT be your partner in fostering a culture of continuous improvement and professional growth, empowering you to become an even more effective and reflective educator.

Maximizing ChatGPT's potential in managing professional responsibilities offers numerous benefits for educators. By embracing AI-powered prompts, teachers can enhance their efficiency, collaboration, resource access, time management, and reflective practice. As we transition to the next section, where we explore case studies and examples of teachers successfully utilizing ChatGPT, remember to harness the power of AI to unleash your full potential in managing your professional responsibilities.

Interactive Discussions With ChatGPT For Addressing Professional Challenges

In this section, we will explore how interactive discussions with ChatGPT can help teachers address professional challenges related to their responsibilities. By engaging in conversations with ChatGPT, teachers can gain valuable insights, strategies, and innovative approaches to overcome these challenges effectively. The benefits of interactive discussions with ChatGPT are numerous. Teachers can tap into the power of AI to access instant guidance, receive personalized recommendations, and explore new perspectives on managing their professional responsibilities. Through these interactive discussions, teachers can find support and inspiration to navigate the complexities of their roles more efficiently.

Challenge 1: Time Management and Work-Life Balance: Balancing professional responsibilities with personal well-being and maintaining a healthy work-life balance can be a daunting challenge for teachers. It's crucial to prioritize self-care and manage time effectively to avoid burnout and foster overall well-being. Let's engage in a dialogue with ChatGPT, where a teacher seeks guidance on managing time effectively and finding work-life balance:

Example Prompts/Dialogue:

Teacher: "ChatGPT, how can I optimize my time management to ensure a healthy work-life balance?"

ChatGPT: ChatGPT: "One strategy is to create a daily schedule and prioritize tasks based on urgency and importance. Additionally, setting boundaries, delegating tasks when possible, and incorporating self-care activities can contribute to work-life balance. Would you like more specific suggestions?"

Teacher: "Yes, please. I struggle with prioritizing tasks. How can I determine which tasks require immediate attention?"

ChatGPT: "When assessing tasks, consider deadlines, the impact they have on students' learning, and the resources required. You can also break down larger tasks into smaller, manageable steps. Remember to allocate time for self-care and personal activities. Feedback on these suggestions?"

Teacher: "These suggestions are helpful. I'll start implementing them and see how they work for me. Thank you!"

ChatGPT: "You're welcome! Remember to be flexible and adapt these strategies to your specific needs. Feel free to reach out if you need further guidance."

Challenge 2: Writing Professional Correspondence: Effectively conveying messages through professional correspondence, such as emails, letters, and reports, is essential for effective communication and maintaining professional relationships. However, writing professional correspondence that is clear, concise, and impactful can pose a challenge for many teachers. Let's explore a dialogue between a teacher and ChatGPT, where the teacher seeks guidance and strategies for writing professional correspondence:

Example Prompts/Dialogue:

Teacher: "ChatGPT, how can I improve my written communication skills for professional correspondence?"

ChatGPT: "One approach is to start with a clear purpose and structure your correspondence accordingly. Using concise and specific language, being mindful of the recipient's perspective, and proofreading for clarity can enhance your written communication. Would you like additional tips?"

Teacher: "Yes, please. Sometimes, I struggle with striking the right tone in my emails. Any suggestions on how to maintain professionalism while being personable?"

ChatGPT: "To strike the right tone, consider using a polite and friendly approach without compromising professionalism. Tailor your language to the recipient, and when appropriate, include personal touches to establish rapport. It's also helpful to proofread your message and ensure it aligns with your intended tone. How does this sound?"

Teacher: "These suggestions make sense. I will apply them to my next email and see how it improves my communication. Thank you!"

ChatGPT: "You're welcome! Remember that practice and feedback from your recipients can further refine your written communication skills. Feel free to ask for more guidance if needed."

Challenge 3: Collaborating and Networking with Colleagues: Collaborating and networking with colleagues are vital for professional growth and fostering a supportive educational community. However, building strong professional relationships and engaging in effective collaboration can present challenges for teachers. Engage in a dialogue between a teacher and ChatGPT, focusing on the teacher's inquiry about building strong professional relationships and leveraging collaboration:

Example Prompts/Dialogue:

Teacher: "ChatGPT, how can I foster collaboration and build strong professional relationships with my colleagues?"

ChatGPT: "One way to foster collaboration is by actively seeking opportunities to collaborate, such as joining professional learning communities or attending conferences. Building rapport, being open to diverse perspectives, and effectively communicating your ideas can also contribute to strong professional relationships.

Teacher: "That sounds great, ChatGPT. I'll make an effort to seek out collaboration opportunities and engage with my colleagues. But sometimes, I find it challenging to communicate my ideas effectively during collaborative discussions. Any suggestions?"

ChatGPT: "When participating in collaborative discussions, active listening is key. Take the time to understand others' perspectives before expressing your own ideas. Use clear and concise language to articulate your thoughts and provide supporting evidence when necessary. Additionally, being respectful and open to feedback can foster a positive collaborative environment. How does this resonate with you?"

Teacher: "These suggestions are valuable. I'll practice active listening and work on expressing my ideas more effectively during collaborative discussions. Thank you for the guidance!"

ChatGPT: "You're welcome! Remember that collaboration is a continuous learning process, and each interaction offers an opportunity for growth. If you have any specific collaboration scenarios you'd like to discuss, feel free to provide more details."

As teachers engage in interactive discussions with ChatGPT, they unlock a wealth of valuable insights, strategies, and innovative approaches to address their professional challenges. These discussions become a powerful tool in their arsenal, empowering them to Accelerate their professional growth, Crush their challenges, and Elevate their practice. By leveraging the guidance and support offered by ChatGPT, teachers can navigate the complexities of time management, enhance their written communication skills, and foster effective collaboration with colleagues. Reflecting on the insights and recommendations gained from these discussions, teachers can actively apply them to elevate their professional practice and promote their overall well-being. Through this process, teachers are equipped to A.C.E. their evaluations and maximize their potential in managing professional responsibilities. In the next section, we will delve into strategies for utilizing ChatGPT to further enhance professional growth and development.

Strategies For Utilizing ChatGPT To Enhance Professional Growth And Development

Welcome to this final section of this episode, where we delve into practical strategies that empower teachers to maximize the potential of ChatGPT for continuous professional growth and development. By harnessing the power of ChatGPT, teachers gain access to invaluable insights, resources, and strategies that can truly elevate their teaching practices.

Strategy 1: Action Research and Inquiry-Based Learning: Action research is a dynamic and transformative approach to professional growth and development, allowing teachers to investigate and address real-world challenges in their classrooms. ChatGPT can be your trusted companion in this journey, providing guidance and support as you design and conduct action research projects while engaging in inquiry-based learning.

ChatGPT can help you refine your research questions, suggest data collection methods, and provide insights on analyzing your findings. Additionally, ChatGPT can share a range of examples of inquiry-based learning activities that have proven successful in other classrooms, empowering you to incorporate these proven strategies into your own teaching practice.

Example Prompt:

Teacher: "ChatGPT, I want my students to actively monitor their own progress in achieving the instructional goals in *[Subject]* for *[Grade Level]*. How can I foster self-assessment and student participation in the development of assessment criteria?"

Prompt 1: "ChatGPT, how can I effectively utilize AI prompts to guide my action research project and gather meaningful data?"

ChatGPT will provide you with strategies on how to use AI prompts to refine your research questions, gather relevant and meaningful data, and analyze the findings for valuable insights.

Example Prompt:

Teacher: "ChatGPT, I want my students to actively monitor their own progress in achieving the instructional goals in *[Subject]* for *[Grade Level]*. How can I foster self-assessment and student participation in the development of assessment criteria?"

ChatGPT will provide you with a diverse range of examples, including hands-on experiments, project-based learning tasks, and collaborative activities, all of which have demonstrated success in various classrooms. These examples will inspire you to implement inquiry-based learning approaches in your own teaching practice, fostering curiosity and critical thinking among your students.

Strategy 2: Personalized Professional Development Planning

Personalized professional development is crucial for addressing individual needs and goals in your teaching practice. With ChatGPT as your partner, you can create a customized professional development plan tailored to your specific areas of interest and growth. ChatGPT can provide recommendations, resources, and insights that align with your professional goals, enabling you to embark on a personalized learning journey.

By engaging with ChatGPT, you can explore a wide range of professional development opportunities, such as online courses, webinars, conferences, and relevant publications. ChatGPT will assist you in setting goals, tracking your progress, and suggesting strategies for maximizing your learning experience. With ChatGPT as your virtual guide, you can stay updated with the latest research, pedagogical approaches, and innovative practices in education.

Example Prompt:

Teacher: "ChatGPT, what are some recommended professional development opportunities aligned with my interests and goals?"

ChatGPT will provide you with personalized recommendations based on your identified areas of interest and professional goals. These recommendations may include specific courses, conferences, webinars, or research materials that can enhance your knowledge and skills in those areas.

Example Prompt:

Teacher: "How can ChatGPT support me in tracking my progress and ensuring I make the most of my professional development activities?"

ChatGPT will offer strategies for setting measurable goals, monitoring your progress, and reflecting on your professional development activities. It can provide suggestions on how to leverage AI prompts to engage in self-assessment, document your learning journey, and make adjustments to your plan as needed.

Strategy 3: Mentoring and Peer Collaboration: Mentoring and peer collaboration are powerful avenues for professional growth and development, and ChatGPT can serve as your virtual mentor and collaborative partner. Whether you're seeking guidance, feedback, or suggestions for improvement, ChatGPT is there to support you on your journey.

Engaging in mentoring conversations with ChatGPT allows you to explore various teaching scenarios, seek advice on specific challenges, and receive insights on effective instructional strategies. ChatGPT can share examples of successful mentoring experiences, offer perspectives on different teaching approaches, and help you develop innovative practices. Additionally, ChatGPT can facilitate peer collaboration by simulating interactions with other educators. You can engage in virtual discussions, exchange ideas, and co-develop teaching materials or projects. By leveraging ChatGPT's vast knowledge base and conversational abilities, you can expand your professional network, foster collaborative relationships, and benefit from diverse perspectives.

Example Prompt:

Teacher: "ChatGPT, how can I engage in mentoring conversations with you to receive guidance and feedback on specific teaching challenges?"

ChatGPT will provide prompts for initiating mentoring conversations. It can offer advice on structuring your inquiries, seeking specific feedback, and exploring alternative approaches. Through these interactions, you can gain valuable insights and perspectives to enhance your teaching practice.

Example Prompt:

Teacher: "Can you facilitate a virtual discussion with other educators where we can collaborate and exchange ideas?"

ChatGPT will create a simulated dialogue where you can engage in virtual discussions with other educators. It will present prompts and encourage you to share your ideas, seek feedback, and collaborate on various topics. This interactive experience will help you broaden your professional network and benefit from the collective wisdom of your peers.

Strategy 4: Reflective Practice and Feedback Loop: Reflective practice is a vital component of professional growth and development, allowing teachers to critically analyze their teaching experiences, identify areas for improvement, and make informed decisions to enhance their practice. ChatGPT can support you in engaging in reflective dialogues and establishing a feedback loop to foster continuous improvement.

By engaging in reflective conversations with ChatGPT, you can explore your teaching experiences, evaluate the effectiveness of your instructional strategies, and identify areas where you can grow and develop. ChatGPT can provide prompts and thought-provoking questions to guide your self-reflection, encouraging you to analyze your teaching practices, assess student outcomes, and consider alternative approaches. Furthermore, ChatGPT can act as a feedback partner, providing insights and suggestions based on your reflections. It can offer perspectives on instructional techniques, classroom management strategies, and assessment methods. Through this feedback loop, you can refine your teaching approaches, experiment with new ideas, and measure the impact of your pedagogical choices.

Example Prompt:

Teacher: "ChatGPT, how can I engage in reflective conversations with you to analyze my teaching experiences and identify areas for improvement?"

ChatGPT will provide prompts and questions to guide your reflective conversations. It can help you analyze your teaching practices, reflect on student engagement and learning outcomes, and explore ways to enhance your instructional strategies.

Example Prompt:

Teacher: "Can you provide feedback on my lesson plans and instructional approaches based on my reflections?"

ChatGPT will offer feedback on your lesson plans and instructional approaches. It can suggest alternative methods, highlight areas of strength, and provide insights to help you refine your teaching practice. This feedback loop with ChatGPT will enable you to make informed decisions and continuously improve your pedagogy.

In conclusion, the strategies for utilizing ChatGPT to enhance professional growth and development empower teachers to embrace continuous improvement and innovation in their practice. Through action research, personalized professional development planning, mentoring and peer collaboration, and reflective practice with a feedback loop, teachers can harness the power of ChatGPT to gain insights, resources, and support that elevate their teaching effectiveness.

By incorporating ChatGPT into their professional journey, teachers can A.C.E. their evaluations, cultivating an environment of Adaptation, Collaboration, and Excellence. ChatGPT serves as a trusted companion, providing guidance, suggestions, and inspiration for addressing professional challenges, refining instructional practices, and fostering a culture of continuous learning.

As we move forward, the next and final episode will delve into the best practices and strategies for using ChatGPT effectively in the educational setting. These insights will empower teachers to optimize their interactions with ChatGPT, ensuring maximum benefits for student learning and teacher professional development. Embrace the transformative potential of ChatGPT as we embark on the final episode, where we will explore the Best Practices/Strategies for Using ChatGPT Effectively and unlock new dimensions of educational excellence.

Episode Five
Best Practices/Strategies: Harnessing the Power of AI

Establishing A Productive Relationship With ChatGPT and AI Tools

To maximize the benefits of using ChatGPT in your journey to A.C.E. your teacher evaluation, it's crucial to establish a productive relationship with this AI-powered tool. Here are some best practices to consider:

Building Rapport: Approach your interactions with ChatGPT as if you were building a relationship with a knowledgeable colleague. Use polite language, express gratitude for its assistance, and maintain a respectful tone throughout your conversations.

Setting Clear Objectives: Clearly define the purpose of your interaction with ChatGPT. Whether you seek insights on a specific teaching strategy or guidance on improving student engagement, having clear objectives will help ChatGPT provide more targeted and relevant responses.

Providing Context: Context matters! When engaging with ChatGPT, ensure you provide sufficient background information about your teaching context, grade level, subject area, and any specific challenges you face. This context enables ChatGPT to offer more tailored and insightful recommendations.

Structuring Conversations With ChatGPT For Optimal Outcomes

To ensure optimal outcomes when conversing with ChatGPT, consider the following strategies for structuring your interactions:

Asking Specific Questions: Formulate questions that are clear, concise, and specific. Instead of asking broad inquiries, break them down into smaller, focused queries. This approach helps ChatGPT provide more precise and relevant information.

Providing Examples: When seeking advice on teaching strategies or lesson plans, provide concrete examples to illustrate the specific challenges or areas you want to address. Sharing examples enables ChatGPT to generate more practical and tailored recommendations.

Seeking Diverse Perspectives: Experiment with different prompts and perspectives to broaden your insights. ChatGPT can provide alternative viewpoints, offer innovative approaches, or challenge your assumptions. EmbrA.C.E. the opportunity to explore various angles to enhance your teaching practice.

Incorporating ChatGPT Feedback Into Teaching Practice

Effectively incorporating ChatGPT feedback into your teaching practice can greatly enhance your performance in teacher evaluations. Consider these strategies:

Reflecting on Feedback: Take time to reflect on the feedback and suggestions provided by ChatGPT. Consider how it aligns with your existing teaching methods and philosophies. Evaluate the potential impact of integrating the recommendations into your classroom practice.

Adapting and Personalizing: Adapt the AI-generated suggestions to fit your unique teaching style, students' needs, and the specific requirements of your evaluation framework. Personalize the recommendations to ensure they align with your teaching philosophy and classroom dynamics.

Iterative Implementation: Implement changes gradually and iteratively. Incorporate the recommended strategies or modifications into your teaching practice, observe the outcomes, and make adjustments as needed. This iterative approach allows for continuous improvement and refinement over time.

Overcoming Challenges And Limitations Of Using ChatGPT

While ChatGPT is a valuable tool, it's essential to be aware of its limitations and address any challenges you may encounter:

Critical Evaluation: Apply critical thinking when interpreting ChatGPT responses. While it can provide valuable insights, remember that it's an AI model and may not always generate perfect, unbiased or contextually appropriate suggestions. Use your professional judgment to assess and validate the information received.

Collaboration and Human Expertise: ChatGPT should complement, not replace, human expertise and collaboration. Engage in conversations with colleagues, mentors, and other educators to discuss ChatGPT-generated ideas, gather diverse perspectives, and enhance your teaching practices through collective intelligence.

Ethical Considerations: Be mindful of ethical considerations surrounding AI use. Respect student privacy, ensure appropriate data usage, and adhere to your school's policies and guidelines when using ChatGPT. Maintain ethical practices in all aspects of incorporating AI technology into your teaching.

By following these best practices and strategies, you can effectively leverage ChatGPT to enhance your teaching practices, gather valuable insights, and A.C.E. your teacher evaluation. Remember to establish a productive relationship, structure conversations for optimal outcomes, incorporate feedback into your teaching practice, and address challenges and limitations with a critical and ethical mindset. Harness the power of ChatGPT as your AI assistant and embark on a transformative journey towards achieving teaching excellence and success in your evaluations. Let ChatGPT be your guide, supporting you in reaching your full potential as an educator and positively impacting student learning outcomes. Together, with ChatGPT, you can A.C.E. your teacher evaluation and create a classroom environment that fosters growth, engagement, and exceptional educational experience.

Recap Of The Benefits Of Integrating ChatGPT to A.C.E. your Evaluation

Throughout this series, we have explored the powerful role that ChatGPT plays in assisting teachers to A.C.E. their teacher evaluations. Let's recap some of the key benefits:

Instant Insights and Time-saving Strategies: ChatGPT provides instant access to valuable insights, time-saving strategies, and innovative approaches that accelerate your professional growth and improve student outcomes. By leveraging AI prompts, you can quickly gain access to a wealth of knowledge and resources.

Tailored Recommendations: ChatGPT offers personalized recommendations aligned with the evaluation framework, enabling you to enhance your teaching practices in specific areas of concentration. Its ability to provide targeted guidance ensures that your efforts are focused on areas that matter most for your evaluation success.

Unlocking Hidden Strategies: By engaging with ChatGPT, you have the opportunity to uncover hidden teaching strategies, overcome evaluation challenges, and decode effective practices that can significantly impact your performance in the classroom and evaluation settings.

Encouragement For Continued Growth And Exploration

As you conclude this A.C.E. E-Book Series, we want to encourage you to continue your growth and exploration as an educator. Here are a few words of encouragement:

Embrace Lifelong Learning: Teaching is a dynamic profession, and there is always room for growth and improvement. Embrace a mindset of lifelong learning, seeking out new ideas, approaches, and technologies that can enhance your teaching practice.

Collaborate and Share: Engage in collaborative discussions with fellow educators, both within and beyond your school community. Share your experiences with using ChatGPT, exchange ideas, and learn from one another. Collaboration can enrich your teaching journey and contribute to collective growth.

Reflect and Iterate: Take time to reflect on your experiences with ChatGPT and the insights gained. Use this knowledge to iterate and refine your teaching practices, making continuous improvements that benefit both you and your students.

Final Thoughts And Closing Remarks

In closing, we want to express our admiration for your dedication to excellence in teaching. The journey to A.C.E. your teacher evaluation is an ongoing process, and integrating ChatGPT into your practice is a powerful tool that can propel you towards success.

Remember, ChatGPT is not a magic solution but rather an invaluable resource to support your professional growth and enhance your teaching effectiveness. As you continue your teaching journey, stay open to new possibilities, remain adaptable, and leverage the potential of AI technology responsibly and ethically.

We sincerely hope that this A.C.E. E-Book has provided you with valuable insights, practical strategies, and the confidence to harness the power of ChatGPT in your quest to A.C.E. your teacher evaluation. Your commitment to creating a top-tier classroom culture and environment, supported by the innovative capabilities of ChatGPT, will undoubtedly contribute to exceptional teaching and positive student outcomes.

Thank you for joining us on this transformative journey. Wishing you continued success, fulfillment, and joy in your teaching career.

Keep A.C.E.-ing your evaluations and inspiring the next generation of learners!

While we are confident that the strategies presented in this book will provide valuable insights and support for improving teacher evaluations and practice, it is important to note that individual outcomes may vary. We cannot guarantee specific results or assume liability for any outcomes resulting from the implementation of these strategies. It is recommended that educators exercise their professional judgment and adapt the strategies to their specific contexts and needs.

References

(n.d.). Common Core State Standards Initiative: Home. Retrieved June 5, 2023, from

https://www.thecorestandards.org

(n.d.). Next Generation Science Standards: Home Page. Retrieved June 5, 2023, from

https://www.nextgenscience.org/

Danielson, C. (2011). *The Framework for Teaching Evaluation Instrument*. Danielson Group.

Author Biography

Dr. Taylor Mitchell, popularly known in the AI world as "TechEd Maven", is a seasoned technology integration expert focused on revolutionizing education through STEAM (Science, Technology, Engineering, Arts, and Mathematics). She holds various certifications across multiple states, including Science/Special Education Teacher, Teacher Evaluator, Principal, and Superintendent of Schools, and possesses an earned doctorate in Educational Leadership.

With over twenty years of educational experience as a teacher, Instructional Coach, School Leader, and District Administrator within one of the nation's largest school systems, Dr. Mitchell is poised to support educators at all levels of their career with research-based strategies for improving practice.

With a background in STEAM, instructional/school leadership, and a passion for educational innovation, Dr. Mitchell helps educators and educational leaders navigate the ever-evolving landscape of educational technology. Through her practical guidance, engaging resources, and hands-on workshops, she equips educators with the knowledge and skills to effectively leverage AI and tech tools. Her mission is to ensure that classrooms become dynamic environments that foster creativity, critical thinking, and digital literacy.

To learn more about Dr. Taylor Mitchell and her work, please follow her on Amazon, connect on LinkedIn or visit www.TechEdMaven.com.

Made in the USA
Middletown, DE
06 September 2023

38060003R00066